INSIDE THE FOOD PROCESSOR

**Tips,
Tricks
and
Terrific Recipes**

by
Maxine Horowitz

Cover Design by Louis Nardo
Illustrations by
Louis Nardo and Judy Levy

Good Food Books

Table of Contents

Introduction

The year 1978 will be a year long remembered by people interested in the preparation of food. It was the year that the food processor came of age.

Pioneered by the French-made Cuisinart Food Processor, all the major American small appliance manufacturers developed their versions of this phenomenal food processor which combines the functions of the blender, mixer, salad maker, meat grinder and chef's knife in one compact unit.

What makes this type of machine so incredible? Why are men and women rushing into the kitchen instead of to restaurants? This machine is the answer! The speed and precision with which it operates make it a labor saver, par excellence.

Until the Americans began to manufacture the food processor, the hefty price tag on the French-made model made ownership a luxury. Serious cooks, however, continued to find that the cost was well worth the sacrifice. Now, the domestic food processors are affordable by cooks everywhere.

As you leaf through most of the cookbooks written for the food processor, you will notice that they are dominated by exotic recipes and "company" meals. Two pages of canape butters or five varieties of mayonnaise just won't do when you're left with an hour until supper and you haven't been to the market in days! This book is designed with you and your schedule in mind. Most of the recipes can double for entertaining and everyday family meals. Many can be prepared ahead or frozen. The majority of these recipes are favorites of students in my regular cooking classes. I have adapted them for use with the food processor. The following pages will give you specific hints and safety tips for proper operation and uniform results. *Read these pages carefully.* If you have not been able to attend one of my classes or see a demonstration on the use of the machine, these pages are even more important. Construction and operation are simple, but proper techniques are crucial for good results.

Before you start, examine the parts of the machine.

PARTS OF THE MACHINE

A. **Motor Base.** The steel or *Lexan* ® housed motor base is the source of power for your food processor. All machines, whether direct drive (as are the ones shown in this book) or belt driven, are equipped with a drive shaft extending from the center of the base. You will notice that all the machines have an indented dot on the front of the base. In many cases this dot becomes your ON/OFF switch. In some of the more recent or "second generation" machines there is an actual switch to activate the motor. These newer machines also have a "PULSE" or "FLASH" switch which enables you to rapidly turn the machine on and off to chop, a technique done with a twist of the wrist in the "1st generation" machines.

The motor on the food processor is sealed so you need not worry about shocks. It is not immersible and thus should only be wiped down with warm soapy water.

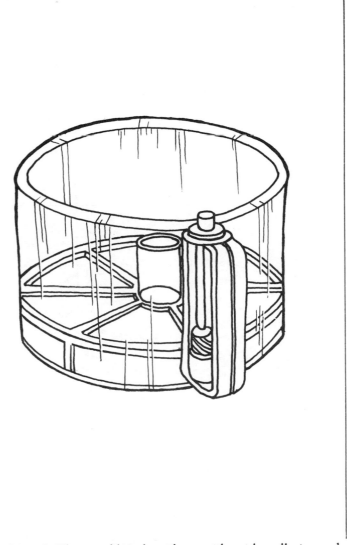

B. **Workbowl.** The workbowl, with or without handle is made of Lexan® , a shatterproof plastic that is used for airplane windows. On the side of the bowl you will notice a stem protruding. This contains a spring action which when in place over the dot on the front of the base, will activate the motor. In the case of machines with manual switches placement of the bowl will prepare the machine to be started.

The bowl, as well as the cover, blades and spatula are dishwasher proof. It is preferable to wash these parts by hand using a soft sponge or brush. You may air or towel dry these parts.

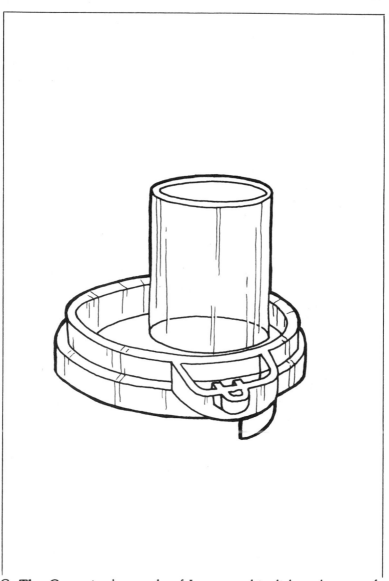

C. **The Cover** is also made of *Lexan* and is dishwasher proof. Protruding from the top is the *feed tube* where much food is processed and the only way to add ingredients while the machine is in operation. On the edge of the cover, just below and to the left of the feed tube you will find a small extension. If you own a machine without external switches this piece must be pushed in place over the stem of the bowl to engage the motor. This same method is used when machines are equipped with manual switches. Once the bowl and lid are completely in place the switch will start the motor.

D. **The Pusher** is used to guide food through the feed tube into the slicing or shredding disks. *It is not dishwasher safe.* This piece should also be used when processing liquids or flour in order to eliminate splashback. *Always use the pusher, never your fingers to push food through the feed tube.*

The design of each pusher is slightly different. Some have open tops, others are closed. Several with open tops are calibrated so that you can use them as a one cup measure.

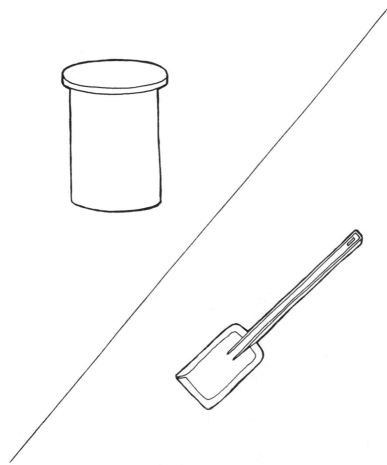

E. **The Spatula** is used to scrape food from the sides of the workbowl. The firm plastic construction enables you to clean out the bowl with little effort. *Never try to use the spatula while the food process is operating.*

These are the basic parts of the machine. Before a description of each blade and its function is presented it is important to have an explanation of the principles of operation.

OPERATION

The machine should be plugged into a 120 volt electrical outlet and placed on a firm surface. Be sure to use a properly grounded outlet, unless the cord is double insulated. You should stand your machine in a convenient place on the counter, (always store it unplugged) with the front facing you. Place the workbowl over the drive shaft with the vertical stem just slightly to the left of the indented dot, or the line on the base. Push the bowl into place over the dot with your hands. *If the bowl is not exactly in place the machine will not start.* Each machine has a slightly different method for locking the bowl into place. If you see that the method suggested here does not work with your machine then refer to your owner's manual. Place one of the blades or disks in place over the drive shaft and spin it slowly with your fingertips until it slips down and locks in place.

If your machine is equipped with a pulse switch you will PULSE wherever you see a reference to on/off. The pulse replaces a manual turn of the wrist. Machines vary in the length of the pulse so you will have to experiment with different types of foods until you get the desired results.

Next, place the cover on the bowl with the feed tube just to the left of the vertical stem. Place your hand on the side of the feed tube and turn the entire cover to the right, pulling the plastic lip extending below the rim of the lid into place over the vertical stem. This will push the spring down. When the spring is depressed it activates the motor. In order to stop the machine you must move the lid to the left, out of place, and allow the spring to be released.

If your machine has the on/off switch, the lid must be securely in place before the switch will go on. (The lid should never be removed while blade is spinning). This is the off position. *Your machine should always be stored in the off position.*

BLADES AND THEIR USES

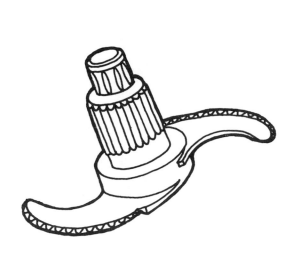

Steel Blade

The double sided steel blade is your most versatile tool. It will do the function of a blender, mixer, and meat grinder. Hard foods or ice cubes should be added through the feed tube which you can over cover with your hand between additions.

There are times when the processing will be very loud. As the pieces get chopped the noise decreases. If the machine starts to move on the counter, place your hand on the base, and again, as the pieces become smaller, the movement will stop. Do not put more than 2 cups of food in the workbowl to be chopped with this blade as it may create uneven results.

There are several techniques that must be learned in order to operate the machine in a satisfactory manner. The first is the ON/OFF method. This refers to a quick wrist motion which turns the machine on, then off immediately. This method gives you control of results. The processor works so quickly that you must check the bowl after one or two on/off turns, particularly if you are chopping soft foods like mushrooms or onions.

The second technique is to let the machine run to mix, knead dough, puree, or process foods which need time, such as mayonnaise or peanut butter.

The third technique is dropping food through the feed tube while the machine is operating. This technique is used for mincing small quantities of food such as 1 or 2 cloves of garlic, for crushing ice, or grating hard cheeses like parmesan. In addition, you may add food to a recipe already being processed in the workbowl, i.e. adding eggs or flour to cake batter.

To chop firm vegetables (potatoes, carrots, turnips)

Cut the food into pieces no larger than 1-1/2" on a side. Place up to 2 cups of cubes into the workbowl with the blade in place. Turn the machine on and off quickly several times using the feed tube as a handle. Check to see if the pieces are the desired size. Continue turning the machine on and off until the pieces are the required size. *This is most important for controlling the size and texture of the food you are processing.* Using this method also allows pieces of food which have been thrown up the sides of the bowl, to drop down close to the blade and be processed.

To chop soft vegetables (onions, scallions, peppers)

Be sure onions are halved or quartered and other vegetables are in chunks no large than 1-1/2"-2". Use a very fast on/off turn once or twice and then check. Soft vegetables process quickly and if you let the machine run you will extract the juices. If the vegetables are processed properly there should be a minimum of juice in the bowl.

To chop parsley or other herbs

Be sure the blade and bowl are dry. Put a large or small amount of greens in the bowl, with or without stems, and process using the on/off method. Store in a closed container in the refrigerator.

To chop raw meat

Cut cold or partially frozen meat into 1" cubes and remove loose fat and gristle. Place up to 1/4 lb. of cubes into the workbowl and using the on/off method chop until the desired fineness is achieved. Remove cover to check texture. If you find the meat catching on the blade, turn the machine on and drop the meat, all at once, through the feed tube and continue to process as directed above.

To chop cooked meat

Follow the same procedure as for raw meat. You may chop other ingredients with the meat such as vegetables, herbs, bread crumbs or eggs.

To grate parmesan cheese

In order to get a fine texture, many people like to process this cheese with the steel blade rather than with the grating disk. Be sure that the parmesan or any hard cheese is at room temperature and cut it into 1/2" pieces. Start the machine and add the cubes through the feed tube. Turn on and off several times, then let the machine run until the cheese is finely grated.

To make peanut or other nut butters

Be certain that the blades are covered with nuts. Turn the machine on and off then let the machine run until a paste forms on the side of the bowl. You may want to add a small amount of oil or butter at this time to improve the spreading consistency.

To chop and grind nuts

Place nuts in workbowl and use the on/off method until the nuts are chopped to the desired fineness. A coarse chop will only take a few turns. If you want to grind nuts for a torte, add a small amount of flour from the recipe, and continue to process, checking the bowl every few seconds. DO NOT over process or you will have a nut butter.

To make bread crumbs or cracker crumbs

You may use fresh or stale bread, broken up. French bread should be in smaller pieces as it takes longer to process. Crackers should also be broken up. Use the on/off method until desired texture is achieved.

To beat egg whites

Be sure that the workbowl and blade are clean, dry, and free of grease. Place at least 4 egg whites in the bowl with 1/4 tsp. salt or cream of tartar. Process until the desired stiffness is achieved. Remove whites from the workbowl and gently place in a mixing bowl. Do not try to fold ingredients into the whites in the workbowl or you will lose the volume. You will notice that you have a reduced volume using the food processor for this process. When maximum volume is necessary use an electric mixer.

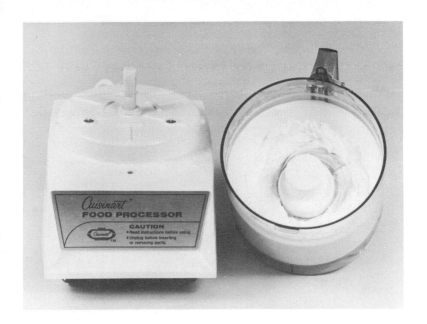

To whip cream

Chill the bowl and blade for 15 minutes. Pour the cold cream into the workbowl. Put the pusher in place and turn the machine on. Remove the pusher to let the air in. After about a minute, or when the cream has thickened to the consistency of sour cream, you can add flavoring through the feed tube. Continue to process until the cream has begun to form a rim on the side of the bowl. You may stop the machine to check. Look through the feed tube; if there is any liquid remaining on the bottom, continue to process. *Don't leave the machine running or you may get butter.* This cream will be heavy and stiff, but will be adequate for toppings.

To make pastry dough

Place dry ingredients in the workbowl with cold shortening or frozen butter that has been cup up. Insert pusher. Turn machine on and off several times to cut the butter to the desired fineness. With the machine running, add liquid through the feed tube. Process only until you see the dough starting to form a ball over the blade. Even if all the dough is not in a ball, stop the machine, and press the loose pieces into the larger mass by hand. *Do not over process or the dough will be tough.* Chill or roll out. Use your favorite recipe, but best results are achieved using no more than 1-1/2 cups of flour at a time. The machine works so quickly you can repeat the operation for a larger quantity, rather than overloading it the first time.

Mixing cakes

It is possible to mix cakes in the food processor. You must bear in mind that the blade does not aerate like a mixer, therefore, light textured cakes are best not done with the machine. Quick breads, other cakes that do not require prolonged beating, or cakes which require separate beating of yolks and whites can be made successfully. It is important to remember that when baking soda is used you must not overprocess or you will get a tough cake.

To make flavored spreads or butters

Place solid ingredients to be chopped in the workbowl. Process using the on/off method until food is finely chopped. Add butter or cheeses and process until smooth. If liquids are to be added, cut down on the quantity until you check the texture of the mixture.

14

Slicing Disk

The **slicing disk** will slice vegetables, cheese, and frozen meat. The basic technique for control with this disk is the amount of pressure exerted on the pusher while the food is being sliced. The heavier the pressure, the thicker the slice. The lighter the pressure, the thinner the slice. It is also important that the food being sliced is wedged firmly in place. If the food is allowed to move freely in the feed tube it will be sliced on an angle and the pieces will not be uniform.

On certain processors, the bottom of the feed tube is slightly wider than the top, so that food that is slightly too large to fit in through the top may be wedged in from the bottom.

To slice round thin vegetables (carrots, celery)

Cut the vegetables in lengths just a little shorter than the feed tube. Be sure that the tops and bottoms are cut straight across. Wedge the pieces in firmly. If you are only slicing one or two stalks of celery, cut the pieces shorter but a uniform length, and wedge in place, insert the pusher and exert the appropriate pressure.

To slice round wide vegetables (zucchini, cucumber)
When you are shopping, learn to select thin vegetables that will wedge more easily into the feed tube. If they are unavailable you may have to trim the sides to fit them in. Again, be sure that the tops and bottoms are cut straight across. A 2" length will insure that the food does not have an opportunity to slip out of place while being sliced.

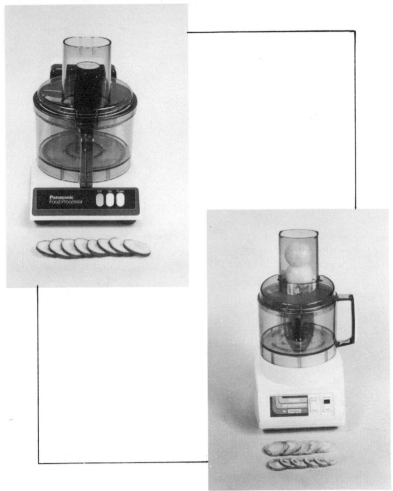

To slice onions
To make onion rings, cut the top and bottom off the onion and wedge in place or push to the right side of the feed tube. Exert firm pressure.

If your onion is too large to go in that way, lay it on its side and slice. If necessary, cut the onion in half lengthwise and wedge the pieces in upright. Exert firm pressure.

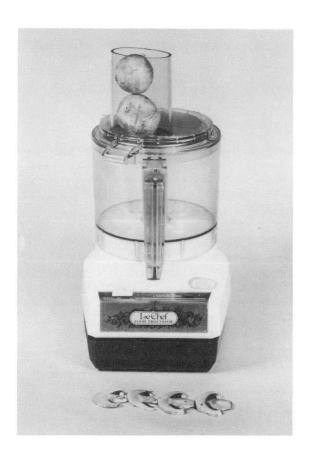

To slice soft fruits and vegetables (mushrooms, strawberries)

Hull berries and remove stems from mushrooms. Fill the feed tube and exert firm pressure. This procedure is used when you have large quantities to process. If you want perfect cross section slices, stand the berries on the blade, hull side down, replace cover and pusher and slice. For the mushrooms, wedge them in on their sides and stack them up. You must exert firm pressure or they will crumble.

To slice cheese or meat

Be sure that the cheese is cold and the meat partially frozen and cut to wedge tightly into the feed tube. Exert very firm pressure with the pusher. **Caution:** All food processors were not designed to do these chores. Those with greater horsepower can do them easily. Other machines may jam. You will have to experiment with your machine to see how these tasks are accomplished.

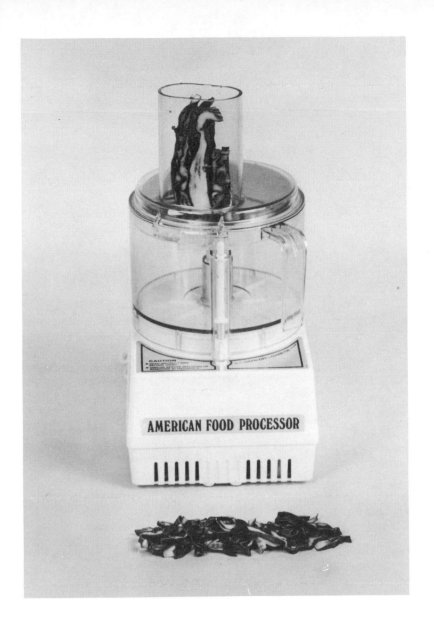

To "shred" cabbage and lettuce

Shop for small, tightly packed heads. Cut into wedges just large enough to force into the feed tube. For the coleslaw most people prefer, exert a very light pressure. For lettuce, use a firmer pressure because it is softer. Be certain that your pusher can be inserted at least a fraction of an inch. If it is not in place you will lose control of your slice.

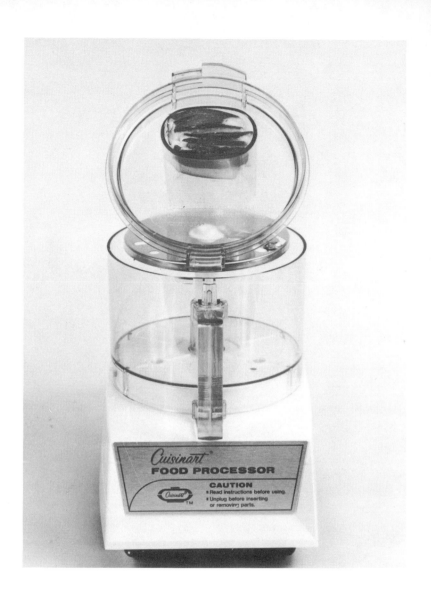

To make vegetables for dip and julienne slices

Insert a section of the wide piece of the carrot or zucchini horizontally into the feed tube. Exert firm pressure to get slices for dipping. Try to pick up the slices and replace them in order, wedging them back tightly into the bottom of the feed tube, cut side facing down. (Move the pusher out of the way several inches with your fingers). Replace the cover carefully, insert the pusher, and exert firm pressure. You will find julienne or matchstick vegetables. If you use round food like potatoes or beets you can use the cross sections to julienne.

The Shredding Disk

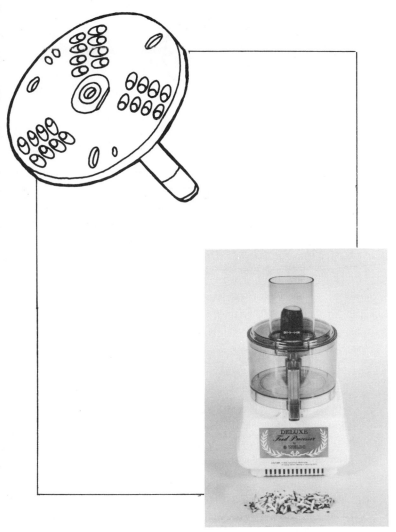

Hard or soft vegetables
If you want a short shred, stand the cleaned vegetable pieces in the feed tube and wedge tightly. If you want long firmer shreds, lay the pieces on their sides and exert firm pressure.

Soft cheeses
When shredding cheese, cut pieces to fit into the feed tube and be sure that it is cold or it will jam the machine. Exert firm pressure with the pusher. You will get long thin shreds.

The Plastic Blade

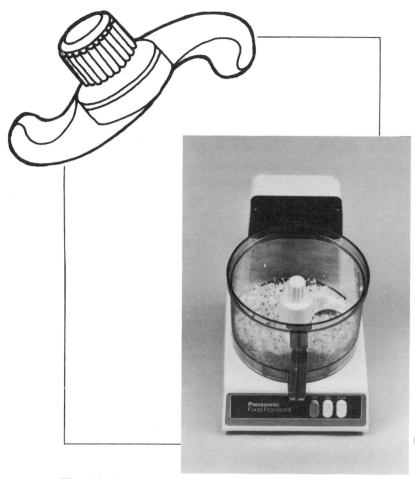

This blade is primarily a mixing blade used for making salad dressing, sauces, and combining ingredients for salads. For example, if you were making tuna salad you would chop your vegetables with the steel blade, then use the plastic blade to combine the chopped vegetables, mayonnaise and tuna. For egg salad cut the eggs in half and place them in the workbowl with the mayonnaise. Use the on/off method for both salads. The use of the plastic blade in conjunction with the on/off method helps control the pulverizing of food.

You might also like to try this blade to mix certain bread doughs. A soft egg dough will mix up very nicely with this blade. The kneading of any recipe containing more than 3 cups of flour should be finished in a larger mixing bowl.

OPTIONAL BLADES & ACCESSORIES

At the present time almost all the manufacturers of food processors produce additional blades and optional accessories, which help achieve the goals of having a food processor replace other space-hungry kitchen appliances and offering an even greater range of cutting and slicing variations. Slicing disks for thick and thin slices are avialable as are a variety of ripple cut and french fry disks. These blades enable the cook, using the same techniques described previously, to create fancy cut foods in the same simple manner.

In most cases if you own a fine slicing disk or other accessory blades you can interchange them where suggested in a recipe to give more variety. For example, try a ripple cut cucumber where a sliced one is suggested.

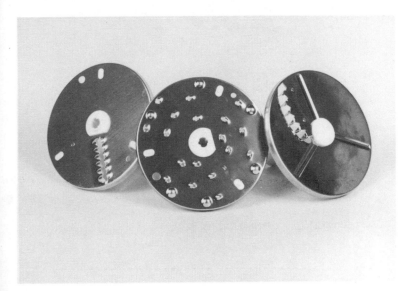

Accessory blades by Cuisinart.

Recently the manufacturers have outdone themselves creating the ultimate in accessories for the food processor owner. One of the most unusual and most welcome items is the potato peeling attachment for the Panasonic, which also will peel apples, onions, and grate orange rind. The vegetable sits on a disk at the top of the unit and a high dome replaces the standard lid. The vegetables are bounced around within the space and the peelings fall into the workbowl. If you are fortunate enough to have the french fry blade for this machine, french fries will frequently be on your menu.

Potato peeler by Panasonic.

Citrus lovers will be pleased to know that there is an accessory incorporating the functions of various kitchen appliances. At present there are a wealth of accessories to help us along, which will allow us to use the processor as a juicer as well. Welco has designed both a citrus juicer and vegetable juice extractor, which fit not only their unit but the two standard size Cuisinart units.

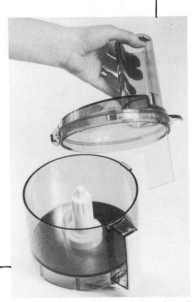

Citrus juicer by Welco.

The Whip By Waring.

One problem which always restricted the use of the food processor for whipping was limited aeration. Waring has devised an attachment which enables the cook to get full volume with egg whites and whipped cream. The whip incorporates air into the mixture with a paddle instead of cutting it out with the chopping blade.

The logistics of preparing and storing sliced and shredded food has always been a bit tricky. A battery of bowls and containers could fill the kitchen until food preparation was completed. The newest accessory on the market is the Insert-a-Bowl, a set of 2 liner bowls for the standard size machines which fit inside the regular bowl. Slice and shred into these plastic bowls, remove and set aside, or cover and refrigerate with the airtight lids, which are included. The workbowl remains clean and you can see how much and what you have processed. A must for Chinese cooking!

Insert-a-Bowl.

Once you get past the vegetable slicing stages into serious cooking and baking, a funnel is a must. There are several types available, with and without the narrow tube extension. The funnel with the tube and pusher is somewhat more useful since you can slice one carrot or banana, or even strawberries without arranging them. For cooking and baking the wide mouth of the funnel enlarges the feed tube and makes adding liquids and flour while the machine is running neater and tedious. The funnels without the tube, made by several of the machine manufacturers, give you the convenience of the latter.

Funnel with pusher.

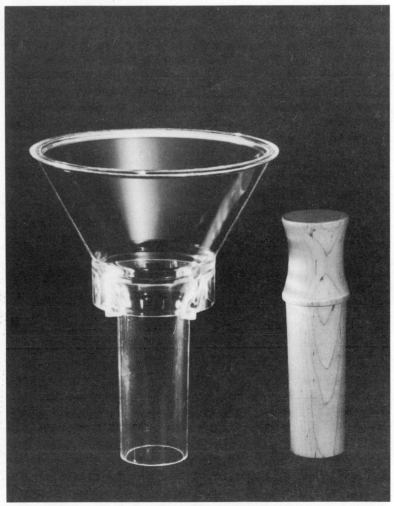

One of your most important purchases should be a storage rack for your basic and accessory blades. It is vital that you store these out of the reach of children and in a place where they are both visible and accessible. Think of them as sharp knives and store them accordingly. There are many racks available holding from 4-8 blades, with a choice of either countertop or wall models. They are available in most department stores and gourmet shops that carry the food processors.

Cuisinart 8 Blade Holder left.
Acrylic Designs Universal Blade Holder right.

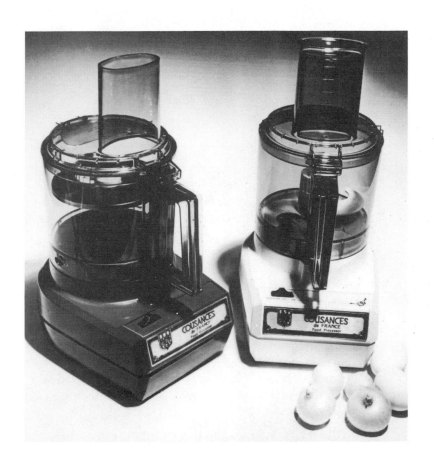

The Newest Star

At press time we became aware of a new machine which will be on the market by late spring of 1979. Presented by Cousances de France, a leader in gourmet cookware, this machine will be found predominantly in gourmet and cookware shops and will offer the serious cook the quality previously reserved for higher priced a mass market machines. If you're in the market to purchase a new machine or change to a more up to date model, check with your local cookware shop for more information.

Revision of Recipes

After many years in the kitchen most cooks develop a repertoire of favorite recipes which they have prepared in the traditional manner, with hand grating of potatoes, endless and tearful mincing of onions, etc. With a small investment of time and thought food processor owners can revise and adapt their own recipes and those from standard cookbooks.

When you have a recipe with many varied ingredients, think about the ones the machine can process for you. If a recipe for stuffing calls for bread crumbs, parsley and onion, for example, the machine can do it all, without washing the bowl between processes. The trick is to start with your driest ingredients first, (bread crumbs) remove them from the bowl, then process the ones with more moisture (parsley) and end with the ones which will be the wettest or which will keep other ingredients from chopping properly. If you started with the onion, for example, the bowl would have to be wiped out before bread crumbs or parsley could be done.

Bakers are also accustomed to softening butter to room temperature before using it for baking. This is not only unnecessary when using the processor but not recommended because the soft butter will be thrown up the sides of the bowl and will have to be scraped down. Using butter straight from the refrigerator, or at room temperature for about 10 minutes will give you the best results.

In very short order you will find that you no longer have to limit yourself to a special processor cookbook. Of course the recipes in this book will make it a prominent member of your cookbook library and one to which you will refer frequently.

Hors d'Oeuvres,

Dips
and
Spreads

Avocado Yogurt Dip

1 medium, ripe avocado, peeled and cut in 1-1/2" chunks
1/2 cup plain low fat yogurt
1/2 tsp. salt
1 tsp. worcestershire sauce

Insert steel blade. Add all ingredients to workbowl, turn on/off several times until large pieces are gone, then process until smooth. Serve with crackers or vegetables as a dip.

Chopped Liver Spread

1 lb. chicken livers
2 large onions, quartered
1/2 cup chicken fat or salad oil
6 hard boiled eggs, halved
salt and pepper to taste

Insert steel blade. Place quartered onions in workbowl and turn on/off 2 times. Place coarsely chopped onion in skillet with heated oil. Saute several minutes, then add livers and cook on medium heat until inside of liver is no longer pink. Cool 10 minutes.

Place half of liver and onions and half of eggs in workbowl with **steel blade.** Turn on/off 4-5 times or until liver is finely chopped. Remove from workbowl. Repeat with remaining ingredients. Season with salt and pepper. Chill. Serve with crackers.

Orange Cheese Dessert Spread

8 oz. cheddar cheese
3 oz. package cream cheese
2 tbs. orange liqueur
1/2 tsp. dry mustard
dash cayenne

Insert shredding disk. Shred cheddar cheese into workbowl. **Insert steel blade,** making sure that no cheese is under the blade. Add remaining ingredients. Process until all ingredients are combined. Pack mixture into a 2 cup oiled mold or form into a ball. Cover tightly with plastic wrap and chill. Unmold.

For full flavor, allow cheese to stand at room temperature before serving. Serve with fresh sliced fruits and crackers.

Herbed Cheese Spread

1 clove garlic
1 full sprig of parsley, stem removed
4 scallions, trimmed to 6" lengths
11-12 oz. cream cheese
salt and pepper to taste

Insert steel blade. Process scallions, garlic and parsley until finely minced. Cut cream cheese into 2 oz. pieces and place in bowl. Turn machine on and process until the mixture is soft and creamy. If necessary, stop machine and scrape down sides to include pieces of greens that are stuck to sides. Season with salt and pepper.

Appetizer Cheese Cake

1 cup cheese crackers
1 cup sour cream
1/4 of a green pepper
1 small rib of celery
1/4 tsp. worchestershire sauce
6 pimento olives
2 tbs. onion
1 tsp. lemon juice
2-3 drops pepper sauce
paprika

Insert steel blade. Process crackers until fine crumbs form. Measure 2/3 cup. Set aside. Cut pepper into 1-1/2" pieces and chop finely using on/off method. Measure 1/4 cup. Cut celery into 1-1/2" pieces and mince using 4-5 on/off turns. Set aside. Chop olives finely using on/off turns.

Line 2-1/2 cup bowl with plastic wrap. Combine all ingredients but crumbs. Spread 1/3 of mixture on bottom of bowl. Add 1/4 cup crumbs. Repeat layers. End with sour cream layer. Chill overnight. Turn out on serving plate and top with additional crumbs. Serve with vegetables or crackers.

Chili Cheese Log

1 lb. Velveeta cheese, cut into 1-1/2" chunks
1/2 lb. American cheese, cut into 1-1/2" chunks
1/3 cup nuts
1 clove of garlic
chili powder
paprika

With steel blade in place, put nuts in workbowl and chop coarsely using on/off turns. Set aside. **Replace blade,** turn machine on and drop garlic through feed tube and mince.

Add half of cheeses and nuts to workbowl containing minced garlic. Scrape down pieces of garlic. Process until well mixed. Repeat with remaining cheeses. Scrape out of bowl and shape into two rolls.

Combine chili powder and paprika on waxed paper. Roll cheese logs in mixture until coated. Wrap in plastic wrap and chill. These can be frozen.

Cold Eggplant Appetizer

1 medium eggplant
1 cup olive oil
10 cherry tomatoes
1 clove of garlic
1 small onion
1/3 cup pine nuts (pignolia)

Insert steel blade. With motor running drop garlic in feed tube and mince. Quarter onion, add to workbowl and mince. Set onion and garlic aside.

Trim, peel and discard ends of eggplant. Cut into 1/4″ slices. In large skillet, heat 1/3 cup oil and cook eggplant until soft and golden brown, adding more oil as necessary and removing pieces as done. Drain eggplant on toweling and squeeze out excess oil.

Blanch tomatoes in boiling water for 10 seconds. Peel. Quarter eggplant slices and place in workbowl with tomatoes. **Using steel blade** chop, using several on/off turns. Then add onions and garlic and whirl just until combined. Add nuts and whirl once more. Season to taste with salt and pepper.

Chill. Serve with toasted chunks of pita bread or crackers.

Curried Almond Dip

1/4 cup toasted slivered almonds
3/4 package dry onion soup mix
1/2 tsp. garlic powder
1/2 tsp. curry powder
1 pint sour cream

Insert steel blade. Chop almonds using 3-4 on/off turns. **Insert plastic blade.** Add remaining ingredients and whirl until blended. Chill. Serve with crackers.

Pineapple Pecan Cheese Ball

16 oz. cream cheese
1-8¾ oz. can well drained crushed pineapple
1/4 of a green pepper, cut in 1-1/2" pieces
1 small onion
2 cups pecans
1 tsp. Lawry's seasoned salt

Insert grating disk and grate 1 cup pecans. Set aside. Place onion in feed tube and grate. Set aside. **Insert steel blade** and chop pepper finely using several on/off turns. Wipe bowl, and **replace steel blade.** Place remaining 1 cup pecans in workbowl and chop finely, but do not overchop. **Insert plastic blade.** Cut cream cheese into 1" cubes and process until smooth and creamy. Add drained pineapple, pepper, onion, seasoned salt and 1 cup of chopped nuts. Process until combined. Scrape out of workbowl into waxed paper or another bowl. Cover and chill until firm enough to shape — several hours.

Place remaining 1 cup grated nuts on waxed paper, form two balls from cheese mixture and roll in nuts until evenly coated. Wrap in plastic wrap or foil. At serving time, place a marachino cherry on top and serve with crackers.

Another serving idea — cut the top off a small loaf of pumpernickel. Hollow out the loaf and fill it with the cheese mixture. Replace the top.

Roquefort Log

1/2 cup pecans
1/4 lb. cheddar cheese, cut in 1" cubes
1-1/2 cup crumbled Roquefort cheese
8 oz. cream cheese
1 cup toasted flaked coconut

Insert steel blade. Chop nuts with 5 on/off turns. Set aside. Grate cheddar cheese. Add nuts, Roquefort cheese, cream cheese. Process until combined. Chill 1 hour.

Shape into long log. Roll in toasted coconut. Chill 3 hours. Slice and serve on melba toast.

Spinach Nuggets

2   10 oz. packages frozen spinach
2 cups packaged stuffing mix
4 oz. parmesan cheese, cut in 1/2" pieces
6 eggs
3/4 cup butter, softened
salt and pepper

Cook spinach and drain well.

Insert steel blade. Process cheese until finely grated. Set aside.

Insert plastic blade. Pour in eggs and mix well. Add butter, cheese and spinach and combine. Sprinkle stuffing mix over mixture and process, turning on/off, just until crumbs disappear. Season with salt and pepper. Roll into walnut sized balls. Freeze.

Bake frozen on a cookie sheet for 10 minutes at 350°.

Cheese Puffs

1/2 lb. Swiss cheese cut in 1-1/4" cubes
2 oz. parmesan cheese cut 1/2" cubes (room temperature)
1/4 lb. butter cut in four pieces
3/4 cup flour
3/4 tsp. salt
1/8 tsp. cayenne
1/8 tsp. nutmeg

GLAZE

1 egg, beaten with 1 tsp. water (optional)

Preheat oven to 425°.

Insert steel blade. Grate the cheeses until fine. Remove 1/2 cup from bowl. Add the remaining ingredients. Turn the machine on and off several times to blend the ingredients, then turn on and let the machine run until a dough forms on top of the blade. Remove from bowl and form into a ball and chill for 15 minutes. Break off tablespoons of dough and roll into balls. Flatten into a circle about 1/4" thick. Arrange on a cookie sheet leaving space between each one. Brush top with egg and water mixture, sprinkle with remaining cheese. Bake 10 minutes or until puffed and light brown.

Note: If you are planning to freeze these, roll the dough into two logs, wrap tightly. Defrost slightly and slice. Then sprinkle with remaining cheese.

Makes 36.

Lox Canapes

4 oz. smoked salmon
20 oz. cream cheese, cut in 1" cubes
4 scallions, cut to 6" lengths
1 pullman loaf whole wheat bread

Insert steel blade. Cut scallions in 2" lengths. Place in workbowl and mince. Set aside. Wipe bowl. **Replace blade** and mince salmon. Set aside. Cut cream cheese into 1" chunks and place in workbowl. Process until smooth. Then add salmon and scallions and process until well combined.

Trim crusts from bread. Spread mixture on two slices of bread and stack. Place a third slice on top. Continue until filling is used up. Wrap sandwiches tightly in plastic wrap or wax paper and chill. Cut into slices, squares or triangles.

Sandwich Spreads

Marmalade Spread

2 tbs. orange juice
1/2 cup orange marmalade
6 oz. cream cheese cut in 1" cubes
1/2 cup blanched slivered almonds

Insert steel blade. Place all ingredients in workbowl. Process until all ingredients are combined and nuts are chopped - 5-8 seconds.

Chicken Spread

1 cup cooked diced chicken
1/4 of small onion
3 drops tabasco
1/4 tsp. salt
1/2 cup celery cut in 1" pieces
2 tbs. sweet pickle relish
3 tbs. mayonnaise

Insert steel blade. Place all ingredients in workbowl. Process until chicken and celery are chopped. Add more mayonnaise if mixture is too dry.

Have your bakery slice a loaf of white bread (or tinted bread) lengthwise into slices. Remove crusts. Use these spreads, the lox canape filling or other spreads of your choice as fillings. Spread a thin layer on each piece of bread. Roll up lengthwise, wrap in plastic wrap and chill several hours or overnight. Slice in thin rounds.

Olive Quiche

3 eggs
3/4 cup green olives
1 cup sour cream
1/2 tsp. oregano
3 oz. Swiss cheese, cut in 1-1/2" chunks
1 tbs. chives
1/2 tsp. salt
dash cayenne
1 - 9" pie shell, unbaked

Preheat oven to 425°.

Insert steel blade. Place cheese in workbowl and process turning on/off 4-5 times, then allow machine to run until cheese is finely grated. Set aside. **Remove steel blade and insert slicing disk.** Place olives in feed tube and slice. Place in bowl with cheese.

Insert plastic blade. Place eggs in workbowl and process 5 seconds. Stop machine. Add sour cream and turn on/off twice to combine. Add cheese, olives and seasonings and whirl until combined. Pour into prepared pie shell.

Bake 15 minutes, then reduce temperature to 375° and continue baking 25 minutes longer until filling is set. Cool slightly and cut into wedges. Serve warm, not hot.

Rumaki Balls

3/4 cup imitation bacon bits or 8 strips crisply cooked bacon
1 cup parsley leaves
2 scallions, cut to 6" lengths
1 small onion, quartered
1 can water chestnuts
1 lb. chicken livers
2 tbs. oil
2 hard boiled eggs, cut in half
2 tbs. brown sugar
1 tbs. Teriyaki or soy sauce
1/4 tsp. salt
1/8 tsp. powdered ginger
1/8 tsp. garlic powder

Insert steel blade. Process bacon bits until crumbs appear. Set aside. Mince parsley and set aside with bacon bits. Wipe bowl. Chop water chestnuts with 3 on/off turns. Set aside. Chop scallions and set aside. Chop onions and place in a large skillet with oil and chicken livers. Saute until onions are soft and livers are cooked through. Cool slightly. Place in workbowl with **steel blade.** Turn on/off 4-5 times. Add all remaining ingredients except parsley and bacon bits. Turn on/off to combine. Scrape into a bowl and chill 1 hour. Pinch off small pieces of liver and form into a ball. Roll in parsley and bacon bits and chill again. Serve with toothpicks.

Makes 36.

Korean Meatballs

1 small clove garlic
8 water chestnuts
1 scallion, cut in 2" pieces
1-1/2 lb. chuck or round, cut in 1" pieces
2 tbs. soy sauce
2 tsp. sesame oil
2 tsp. sugar
2 small eggs
flour
salad oil

Insert steel blade. Place cut up scallions, water chestnuts and garlic in workbowl. Chop using 3-4 on/off turns. Set aside. Add meat to workbowl in 3 batches using on/off turns until finely ground. Place in bowl with vegetables. Toss in soy sauce, sesame oil and sugar. Roll into 3/4" balls.

Mix eggs in workbowl. Pour into shallow dish. Coat meatballs with flour, then with egg. Heat oil in skillet. Fry until browned. Drain.

Potato Chips

5 large potatoes
oil for deep frying

Insert fine slicing disk. Slice potatoes. Drop in cold water. Drain and dry off. Heat oil to boiling. Drop in slices, one at a time. Cook until brown and curved. Drain and salt to taste.

Amy's Cottage Cheese Quiche

2 9" prepared pie shells (Oronoque Farms is the best frozen pastry available in this area)
2 oz. Swiss cheese
16 oz. dry curd, low fat cottage cheese
6 eggs (or 1-1/2 container Fleischman's Egg Beaters)
2/3 cup milk
1-1/2 tsp. salt
1/8 tsp. white pepper

Optional (1 cup canned french fried onion rings).

Preheat oven to 450°, then reduce heat to 350°.

Prick pie shells and bake 5-6 minutes.

Insert steel blade. Grate Swiss cheese until mealy. Set aside. **Remove steel blade and insert plastic blade.** Add eggs and whirl until blended. Add cottage cheese, milk, salt and pepper. Turn on and off several times until combined. Sprinkle each pie shell with half the Swiss cheese. Pour half the filling over each one. Place on a cookie sheet and bake 45 minutes at 350°.

Remove from oven and sprinkle with onion rings. Return to oven to brown onions, 5-10 minutes.

Cheese Fritters

1/2 recipe of cream puff pastry (page 131)
1/2 tsp. baking powder (add with flour)
2 oz. cheddar cheese cut in 1" cubes
1 oz. Swiss or gruyere cheese cut in 1" cubes
2 egg whites

Hot oil for deep frying.

Prepare cream puff pastry dough. **Insert steel blade.** Process all cheeses until finely grated. Place in bowl with dough. Wash and dry bowl and blade thoroughly. **Reinsert steel blade** and beat egg whites until stiff, several minutes. Fold into dough and cheeses. Blend thoroughly. Drop by tablespoons into hot oil and fry 10 minutes or until golden. Roll in additional grated cheese.

Cheddar Pecan Spread

1/4 cup pecans
1/2 lb. cheddar cheese
1/3 cup mayonnaise
2 scallions, cut in 2" pieces
1 tbs. pimento

Insert shredding disk and shred cheese. **Insert steel blade.** Add mayonnaise and scallions and process until smooth. Add pimento and nuts. Use on/off turns until they are chopped.

Sesame Cheese Wheel

DOUGH

1 package active dry yeast
2/3 cup warm water, 110-115°
2 cups flour
2 tbs. salad oil
1/2 tsp. sugar
1/2 tsp. salt

FILLING

1 beaten egg
3 cups or 12 oz. cold muenster cheese
1/2 cup parsley leaves, washed and dried
1 tsp. garlic salt
1/8 tsp. pepper

GLAZE

1 slightly beaten egg
1 tbs. water
1-1/2 tsp. sesame seeds

Insert shredding disk. Cut cheese to fit in feed tube and with firm pressure shred into workbowl. Set aside in mixing bowl. **Insert steel blade** and place parsley in workbowl. Process until finely minced. Place in mixing bowl. Wipe workbowl. Place egg in workbowl and whirl until mixed. Place in mixing bowl. Add garlic salt and pepper to mixing bowl and combine filling ingredients. Add egg and water to workbowl for glaze. Whirl until combined. Set aside.

In a one cup measuring cup combine water, yeast and sugar. Proof for 5-10 minutes in a warm place.

Insert steel blade. Place 1-1/2 cup flour, salt and oil in workbowl. Add yeast mixture. Turn machine on and process 10 seconds. Very quickly add remaining flour and continue processing for 45 seconds. Dough should be smooth and elastic. Place in lightly greased bowl, turning once to grease surface. Cover, let rise in warm place until doubled, about 1 hour. Punch down, divide into two parts. Cover and let rest 20 minutes.

On lightly floured surface, roll one portion to a 13" circle. Place circle on lightly greased 12" round pan. Spread filling over dough in pan. Roll remaining dough out to a 13" circle. Place over filling. Trim and flute edges. Bake at 400° for 20 minutes. Remove from oven and brush top with reserved egg and water mixture. Sprinkle with sesame seeds and return to oven for 12-15 minutes more. Cut in narrow wedges. Serve hot.

Makes 16-20 servings.

Chinese Egg Rolls

1/2 small head of cabbage, cut in wedges
2 ribs of celery cut in 1-1/2" chunks
2 large cooked chicken breast halves or
2 cups cooked shrimp or pork or a combination
8 scallions
1 can water chestnuts
2 cloves garlic
1/4 cup soy sauce
1 tbs. sugar
1/2 tsp. salt
1/4 tsp. pepper
1 tsp. sesame oil
1 dozen prepared egg roll skins
oil for deep frying

Insert slicing disk and slice cabbage using firm pressure. Set aside.

Insert steel blade and chop chicken that has been cut into chunks using on/off method until no large pieces remain. Wipe bowl. Chop celery, scallions and water chestnuts separately, wiping bowl after processing. Remember to use on/off method. Set aside. Mince garlic while machine is running.

Place celery and cabbage in saucepan with 1 cup of water. Boil for 30 seconds, then drain.

Heat oil in skillet or wok and stir-fry meat and garlic. Add vegetables, toss and stir-fry several minutes. Add seasonings. Chill several hours. Drain excess liquid.

Place 2 tbs. filling in center of each skin and fold up envelope style tucking edges in and sealing last flap with a paste made of 1 tbs. flour and 2 tbs. water.

Heat oil to 375° and deep fry 2 or 3 at a time. When bottom is brown and crisp, turn and continue cooking. Drain on paper towels. Reheat in 400° oven 10 minutes or until crisp. Serve with duck sauce.

Can be frozen after being cooked and cooled.

Spinach Cheese Rolls

1/4 cup olive oil
1 medium onion, quartered

10 oz. package frozen, chopped spinach, defrosted and drained
1/2 lb. feta cheese
6 oz. ricotta cheese, crumbled
1 tbs. fresh dill
4 scallions, 6" long
3 eggs
1/4 cup bread crumbs
1/2 lb. phyllo dough
1/2 cup melted butter

Insert steel blade. Chop scallions and set aside. Add onion and chop with 3 on/off turns. Saute in oil. Add drained spinach and simmer until moisture is gone. Toss in bread crumbs.

Insert plastic blade. Put cheeses and eggs in workbowl and process until combined. Add scallions and dill. Turn on/off once. Add spinach mixture and turn on/off just until combined.

Keep phyllo dough covered in layers as follows: damp dish towel, waxed paper, phyllo, waxed paper, damp towel. Cut sheets into quarters. Brush each sheet with melted butter. Place 1 tbs. of filling 1" from short edge of sheet. Fold the 1" margin over the mixture. Fold long side edges in, overlapping, and roll to end. Use a new 1-1/2" - 2" paint brush or nylon pastry brush for brushing on butter. Place rolls on cookie sheets. Brush tops with butter and bake at 450° for 20 minutes or until lightly brown. Serve warm. If frozen, reheat at 325° for 10 minutes.

Swiss N' Rye Puffs

1/4 cup parsley leaves
1 small onion, halved
1/2 cup mayonnaise
1/2 lb. Swiss cheese, cold and unsliced
1 loaf party rye

Insert steel blade. Place parsley leaves in workbowl and mince, using on/off turns. Place in mixing bowl. **With steel blade still in place,** chop onion finely, using 4-5 on/off turns. Add onion to mixing bowl. Combine mayonnaise with onion and parsley.

Insert slicing blade. Wedge a piece of Swiss cheese firmly in feed tube and slice, using firm pressure.

Toast bread on one side. Spread mayonnaise on untoasted side. Top with a slice of cheese and sprinkle with paprika. Broil 2-3 minutes 4" from the heat.

Cocktail Cheese Apple

3/4 lb. sharp cheddar cheese, cut in 1" cubes
1/4 lb. Swiss cheese cut in 1" cubes
3 oz. cream cheese, cut 1" cubes
1 tbs. prepared mustard
1 tsp. worchestershire sauce
chili powder
cinnamon stick

Insert steel blade. Grate half of Swiss and cheddar cheese until fine. Add half of cream cheese, 1-1/2 tsp. mustard, 1/2 tsp. worchestershire sauce. Process until smooth. Place in a bowl. Repeat with remaining half of ingredients. Combine mixtures and form into the shape of an apple. Roll in paprika. Form a stem with a piece of cinnamon stick. Chill.

Serve at room temperature with crackers.

Mushroom Roll-Ups

4 tbs. butter
4 medium onions, quartered
1 lb. mushrooms
8 oz. cream cheese
salt, pepper, tabasco sauce
1 pullman loaf inexpensive sandwich bread
1/4 cup melted butter

Insert steel blade. Place cleaned mushrooms in workbowl, 1 cup at a time and chop, using 2-3 very fast on/off turns. Remove each batch after chopping and place in skillet with butter. Place onions in the workbowl 2 at a time and chop using 3-4 on/off turns. Add each batch of onions to skillet after chopping.

Saute mushrooms and onions in butter. Add cream cheese and mix until melted. Add salt, pepper and a drop or two of tabasco sauce. Taste and adjust seasoning.

Remove crusts from bread and flatten with a rolling pin.

Place 1 heaping tablespoon filling on each slice of bread and roll up. Cut in halves or thirds and place on cookie sheet, open end down. Brush with melted butter*. Bake 20-25 minutes at 350°.

*If you are freezing these, brush with butter and bake after defrosting.

**Try the American Electric wide grater to grate mushrooms instead of chopping them.

Oriental Beef Turnovers

10 water chestnuts
1 cup drained bean sprouts
1 small onion halved
3/4 envelope beef flavor mushroom soup mix
1/2 lb. ground beef
2 - 8 oz. packages refrigerator crescent rolls

Insert steel blade. Chop water chestnuts with 3 on/off turns. Set aside. Place bean sprouts in workbowl and turn on/off two times. Set aside. Chop onion with 3 on/off turns.

Preheat oven to 375°. In medium skillet brown meat and onion together. When onion is soft add vegetables and soup mix.

Separate crescent dough as package directs. Cut in half, flatten and roll out. Place small spoonful of filling in center of each triangle. Fold over and seal edges. Place on ungreased cookie sheet. Bake 15 minutes. Makes 32.

Serve with Chinese duck sauce.

Deep Fried Walnut Chicken Bits

1/2 - 3/4 lb. walnuts
2 whole chicken breasts, partially frozen and boned
2 egg whites
1 tsp. salt
1/8 tsp. pepper
1/4 cup cornstarch

Insert steel blade. Add nuts to workbowl and chop with 4-5 on/off turns. Set aside.

Cube each breast half into 9 pieces while partially frozen.

Wash and dry bowl and blade. Add egg whites with a pinch of salt and process until soft peaks form. Scrape into mixing bowl. Fold in cornstarch gently until smooth. Place 1/2 cup nuts in shallow dish. Dip chicken pieces in egg white mixture, then into nuts. Add nuts to plate as needed. Heat oil for deep frying (375°) and drop in chicken pieces one at a time, cooking 8-10 at a time. Cook 1 minute or until light brown. Drain and serve with duck sauce.

Makes 36 pieces. This can also be used as one of several main dishes in a Chinese dinner.

Artichoke Squares

1 cup cheddar cheese
1/4 cup fresh parsley leaves
1 medium onion
1 clove garlic
2 jars marinated artichoke hearts
1/4 cup bread crumbs
4 eggs
1/4 tsp. salt
1/8 tsp. pepper
1/8 tsp. oregano
dash tabasco

Insert shredding disk and shred cheese. Set aside. **Insert steel blade.** Mince parsley and set aside. Wipe bowl. Chop onion with 3-4 on/off turns. Set aside. With machine running drop garlic through feed tube and mince. Scrape out and add to onions.

Drain artichokes and pour oil from one jar into large skillet. **Replace steel blade** and chop drained artichokes using on/off turns. (Do not puree.) Heat oil in skillet and saute onions and garlic.

Insert plastic blade. Place eggs in workbowl and mix with 2 on/off turns. Add all remaining ingredients and whirl until combined. Pour mixture into greased 7" x 11" pan. Bake at 325° for 30 minutes. Cool in pan and cut into 1" squares. Serve lukewarm or room temperature.

Shrimp Remoulade

1 full sprig of dill
1 small onion, halved
1 clove garlic
1 cup mayonnaise
1/4 cup olive or vegetable oil
1/4 cup chili sauce or ketsup
1 tsp. celery seed
2 lb. medium shrimp, cooked

Insert steel blade. Mince dill, set aside. Turn machine on. Drop in garlic then onion pieces. Chop turning on/off until finely minced. **Insert plastic blade.** Add remaining ingredients except shrimp, and process until combined. Toss with shrimp in a large bowl. Cover and chill several hours. Serve with toothpicks.

Serves 8 to 10.

Mock Derma

1 - 12 oz. box Ritz crackers or Tam Tams
2 large ribs celery cut in 1-1/2" pieces
2 large carrots cut in 1-1/2" pieces
1 medium onion, quartered
1 stick margarine or butter, melted
1/2 tsp. paprika
1/4 tsp. pepper
1/2 tsp. salt
1/8 tsp. garlic powder

Insert steel blade. Pour entire box of crackers into workbowl and process until fine crumbs form. Place in large bowl. Process celery, carrots and onions in several batches until finely chopped. Add to crumbs.

Pour melted butter and seasoning over crumb mixture and toss with fork until combined.

Shape into 3 - 2" x 6" cylinders and wrap tightly in foil that has been greased or sprayed with a non-stick coating. Bake on a cookie sheet for 1 hour at 350°. Slice into 1/2" rounds.

Serve as a starch with dinner or as an h'ors d'oeuvre.*

Freezes well.

*To use as an h'ors d'oeuvre make narrow cylinders.

Miniature Quiche

BASIC PASTRY

1 cup flour
1/2 tsp. salt
6 tbs. shortening, chilled
2-3 tbs. ice water

Insert steel blade. Place shortening in pieces on blades. Place flour and salt in workbowl. Turn on/off several times until mixture is mealy. With machine running pour water slowly through the feed tube. Continue to process just until the dough begins to form a ball over the blade. Stop machine and gather any pieces which may remain on the bottom of the bowl. Add to ball. Chill if necessary. Roll out on lightly floured board until dough is 1" wider than the edges of an 8" square pan. Line bottom and 1" up the sides with pastry. Be sure all cracks are sealed. Prick all over and bake 10-15 minutes in a 350° oven.

Miniature Quiche

Filling No. 1

BACON or ONION FILLING

1/4 lb. Swiss cheese
1 tbs. flour
3/4 cup half & half
2 eggs
1/4 tsp. salt
1/8 tbs. pepper
4 slices crisply cooked bacon crumbled or
1 large onion chopped and sauteed in 2 tbs. butter

Insert shredding disk. Shred Swiss cheese. Place in mixing bowl and toss with flour. **Insert steel blade** and place quartered onion in workbowl. Turn on/off 4-5 times until coarsely chopped. Saute onion until soft. Set aside. Wipe bowl. **Insert plastic blade.** Place half and half, eggs, salt and peper in workbowl and whirl until combined. Add reserved onions or crumbled bacon. Sprinkle cheese over bottom of prebaked shell and cover with egg mixture. Bake at 325° for 40-45 minutes or until lightly browned. Cool, cut into small squares and serve.

Filling No. 2

OLIVE FILLING

3 oz. Swiss cheese
20 small pimento olives
3 eggs
1 cup sour cream
1/2 tsp. salt
dash cayenne
1/2 tsp. oregano
1 tbs. chives

Insert shredding disk and shred cheese. Set aside. **Insert slicing disk.** Pour olives into feed tube, exert medium pressure, and slice olives. Set aside. **Insert plastic blade.** Place eggs, sour cream and seasonings in workbowl and whirl until combined. Add cheese and olives and combine. Pour into prepared shell. Bake at 425° for 15 minutes. Reduce heat to 375° and bake 25 minutes more until filling is set. Cool slightly and cut into small squares.

Serve warm.

Breads
and
Soups

Hungarian Apple Soup

1 lb. firm ripe apples
2 whole cloves
2 cups water
1/4 tsp. cinnamon
2 tsp. lemon juice
1/2 cup sugar
1/2 cup dry white wine
2 cups milk
1/2 cup heavy cream
2 tbs. flour

Peel, core and halve apples. **Insert slicing disk** and wedge apple halves in. Slice, using firm pressure. Place in a saucepan with cloves, cinnamon, lemon juice and sugar. Simmer until tender. Return to workbowl and puree. Return puree to saucepan. Add the wine and milk, stirring constantly. Remove from the heat. Blend the flour into the cream, then stir into the soup. Return to a boil and simmer 5 minutes. Chill thoroughly before serving.

Scandanavian Cheese and Potato Soup

1/2 lb. Jarlsberg cheese
1/4 cup parsley leaves
6 large potatoes
3 large ribs celery, cut in 2" lengths
3 large onions
1/2 lb. mushrooms
1/3 cup butter
1/3 cup flour
2 cans (10¾ oz.) chicken broth
1 can (10¾ oz.) beef broth
3 cups water

Insert steel blade. Mince parsley. Set aside. Wipe bowl. **Reinsert slicing disk.** Wedge potatoes in feed tube and slice, using very firm pressure. Set aside. Repeat with celery. Set aside. Place onions on their sides and slice. Pour mushrooms in feed tube and slice.

Combine broths, sliced vegetables and water. Cover and simmer 25-30 minutes.

In a small saucepan melt butter and stir in flour. Cook slowly until golden brown. Blend into simmering soup and stir until soup thickens. Season to taste with salt and pepper.

While soup is cooking **insert shredding disk** and shred cheese.

At serving time sprinkle soup with grated cheese and parsley.

Serves 6-8.

Mulligatawny Soup

1 broiler, fryer chicken 3-4 lbs.
1 quart water
1 tbs. salt
1/8 tsp. mace
1/2 tsp. curry powder
1/4 tsp. cloves
5 sprigs parsley
1 medium onion
1 carrot, cut in 2" lengths
1 rib celery, cut in 2" lengths
1 green pepper
1 tart apple
1/4 cup butter
1/3 cup flour
1 - 8 oz. can stewed tomatoes

Insert steel blade. Chop pepper and apple with 3 quick on/off turns. **Insert slicing disk.** Wedge celery and carrot in feed tube and slice. Place onion on its side and slice whole.

In a Dutch oven, combine chicken, water, spices and parsley. Cover and simmer 45 minutes. Remove chicken. Measure broth. If necessary, add water to make 1 quart. Remove skin and bones from chicken and cut meat into small pieces.

Melt butter in Dutch oven and saute onion, carrot, celery, pepper and apple until tender. Remove from heat; stir in flour. Gradually add broth and tomatoes. Add chicken. Heat to boiling, stirring constantly. Boil 1 minute. Cover and simmer 1 hour.

Serve with a spoonful of hot rice on top.

Carrot Vichyssoise

4 medium potatoes
4 carrots, cut to fit feed tube
1 medium onion
3 cups chicken stock
1 cup light or heavy cream
1 tsp. salt
1/8 tsp. pepper
shredded carrots or scallions for garnish

Insert slicing disk. Slice potatoes, carrots and onion into the workbowl. Boil in chicken stock until soft, about 25 minutes.

Insert steel blade. Pour 1/2 of mixture into workbowl and process until smooth. Pour out quickly, holding blade in place with the spatula. Add cream and season to taste with salt and pepper. Repeat with remaining ingredients.

Vichyssoise

2 leeks, white part only
1 small onion
2 tbs. butter
2 large potatoes
2 cups chicken broth
salt to taste
1 cup milk
1 cup heavy cream
chopped chives

Cut ends off potatoes and trim sides to fit into feed tube. **Insert slicing disk.** Wedge leeks in feed tube and slice. Place onion in feed tube and slice. Remove from bowl and saute leeks and onions in butter.

Replace slicing disk and slice potatoes. When onions and leeks are ready, add potatoes, broth and boil 20-25 minutes or until potatoes are tender. Cool 10 minutes. **Insert steel blade** in machine. Pour contents of pan into processor bowl and puree. Return to saucepan. Add milk and 1/2 cup of cream and bring to a boil. Chill. Add remaining cream. Add salt after soup has been chilled. Serve with chives.

Serves 4.

If you wish to double this recipe, be sure you puree in 2 batches or you will get leakage.

Cold Asparagus Soup

1-1/4 lb. trimmed asparagus or
2 - 10 oz. packages frozen asparagus pieces
2 large leeks, white part only
4 tbs. butter
3 cups chicken boullion
1/4 cup flour
1 tsp. salt
1/8 tsp. pepper
2 cups light cream

Insert slicing disk. Wedge asparagus in feed tube and slice, using firm pressure. Place in saucepan with boiling boullion. Cook 3-5 minutes or until soft.

Slice leeks, using firm pressure, and saute in butter. Add cooked asparagus and saute 1 minute. Stir in flour and cook until absorbed. Add boullion, salt and pepper. Simmer 3 minutes.

Insert steel blade. Puree mixture until smooth. (Process in 2 batches.) Pour into large bowl. Stir in cream and chill 4 hours..

Garnish with parsley.

Serves 6.

Gazpacho

1 cucumber, peeled
4 ripe, peeled tomatoes or 1 can (1 lb.) drained
1/2 medium onion
1/2 large green pepper
1 clove garlic
1/4 cup olive oil
1/4 cup wine vinegar
2 cups tomato juice
3/4 tsp. salt
1/8 tsp. black pepper

Cut up cucumber, pepper and onion in 1-1/2" chunks. Combine oil, vinegar, salt and pepper. **Insert steel blade.** Place half the cut up vegetables, half the tomato juice and half the oil and vinegar mixture in the workbowl. Turn on and off several times and then let the machine run until you have the desired consistency. Pour into large bowl. Repeat process with remaining ingredients. Chill four hours.

Serve with croutons or chopped onions, peppers or scallions.

Makes about six cups.

Cranberry Borscht

5 large shallots
1 tbs. butter
1 - 1 lb. can whole beets, cut into 1-1/2" pieces
3 cups fresh cranberries
1/4 cup Madiera
1 tbs. lemon juice
salt and pepper
3 cups chicken broth
sour cream

Insert steel blade. Chop shallots finely and saute in butter. Place cooked shallots in workbowl. Add beets and liquid and process until pureed. Set aside.

Simmer the cranberries in stock about 5-7 minutes. In two batches puree the berries and stock. Force the puree through a seive.

Combine both purees with Madiera and lemon juice. Season to taste with salt and pepper. Serve hot or cold garnished with sour cream.

White Sandwich Bread

1 package dry yeast
1/2 cup warm water, 105-115°
1 tsp. sugar
2 cups flour
1 cup cake flour
1 tsp. salt
1/2 cup warm milk
2 tbs. butter
salad oil

Proof yeast in warm water with sugar until a layer of foam appears (5-10 minutes).

Insert steel blade. Place 1 cup cake flour, 1-1/2 cups regular flour and salt in workbowl. Put cover on. Add yeast mixture through feed tube and turn on/off 3 times to blend. Add milk and butter. Let machine run a few seconds. Check consistency. Dough should be sticky. Quickly, turn machine on, add flour a little at a time as necessary, and knead for 45-60 seconds. Dough should feel smooth. Let rest 5 minutes, then place in a lightly oiled, warmed ceramic or glass bowl. Turn dough so entire surface has been lightly coated with oil. Cover bowl with plastic wrap, then with damp towel.

Let double in bulk in a warm place, 80°, about 1 hour. Roll out on lightly floured board. Roll tightly and place in a 9″ x 5″ x 3″ loaf pan, that has been oiled. Cover with a damp towel. Let rise again.

Bake in a preheated oven at 425° for 30-35 minutes or until loaf is browned.

Corn Sticks

Makes 14 cornsticks

1 cup flour
1 cup cornmeal
1 tbs. baking powder
1 tsp. salt
1 cup milk or buttermilk
2 tbs. melted butter
2 eggs

Preheat oven to 400°.

Insert steel blade. Add dry ingredients to workbowl. Pour butter over. Process until combined. With machine running, pour milk all at once through the feed tube. Add eggs, one at a time and process until combined.

Generously grease a cornstick mold with any fat except butter and spoon batter into mold until 3/4 full. Bake 18-20 minutes until brown and puffy. Remove at once, regrease mold and refill with remaining batter. Serve hot with butter.

7-20-91

Banana Nut Bread

1/2 cup walnuts
3 ripe bananas, cut into 1-1/2" lengths
1/2 cup oil
1 cup sugar
2 eggs
2 cups flour
1 tsp. baking soda   } Sifted together
1/2 tsp. baking powder
1/2 tsp. salt
3 tbs. milk
1/2 tsp. vanilla
cinnamon and sugar

Preheat oven to 350°.

Insert steel blade. Chop nuts with 2-3 on/off turns. Set aside.

Replace steel blade. Place oil and sugar in workbowl. Turn machine on. Add eggs as mixture is combined, drop bananas in through feed tube and process until large lumps are gone. Add milk and vanilla. Remove top and add sifted dry ingredients turning on/off just until combined. Add nuts. Make 2 on/off turns. Pour into greased and floured 9" x 5" x 3" loaf pan. Sprinkle with cinnamon and sugar and bake 55-60 minutes. *Bake full Time!*

Cinnamon Popovers

2 eggs
1 cup sifted flour
1/2 tsp. salt
1 cup milk
1 tbs. melted butter
3/4 tsp. cinnamon

Preheat oven to 425°.

Insert steel blade. Place all ingredients in workbowl and process 2-3 seconds or until just combined.

Pour into heated iron popover pan or glass custards cups, filling them 3/4 full. Bake for 35-40 minutes or until golden.

Main Dishes

Pirozhki

DOUGH

    2 eggs
    1 cup sour cream
    1/2 cup unsalted butter, cut in 4 pieces
    3-1/2 cups sifted flour
    1 tsp. baking powder
    1 tsp. salt

FILLING

    2 medium onions, quartered
    4 tbs. butter
    1-1/4 lb. beef chuck, in 1-1/2" cubes
    1/4 cup parsley leaves
    2 tsp. minced fresh dill
    2 hardboiled eggs, halved
    3 tbs. sour cream

Preheat oven to 400°.

Insert steel blade. Add eggs, sour cream and butter. Process until combined. Add dry ingredients and process until dough forms a ball. Continue to process a few seconds more. Remove from bowl, coat lightly with flour and chill at least 1/2 hour.

Insert steel blade. Mince parsley. Set aside. Place onions in workbowl and chop turning on/off 3 times. Heat butter in skillet and add onions. Chop meat in 3 batches using on/off turns until finely ground. Add meat to skillet and cook until pink disappears.

Wash and dry bowl. **Insert plastic blade.** Chop eggs, using on/off turns. Add eggs, parsley and dill to meat mixture. Add enough sour cream to bind moisture. Season to taste with salt and pepper. Cool filling before using.

Roll out part of the dough on a floured board to 1/8" thickness. Cut 4" or 5" circles with glass or cooky cutter or cut squares of desired size. Brush circles with beaten egg, then place a heaping tablespoon of filling in the center. Bring opposite edges of circle together on top and pinch together tightly and neatly on the edge. Place on greased and floured cookie sheet and bake 15 minutes or until golden brown.

Makes 24 or more.

Sweet and Sour Meatballs

2 lb. chuck in 1-1/2" cubes
1/2 cup matzoh meal or bread crumbs
2 eggs
1/4 cup brown sugar
1 tsp. salt
1/2 tsp. garlic powder
1/2 tsp. onion powder
1/2 cup tomato sauce (Use 16 oz. can, save
    remainder for sauce)

Insert steel blade. Chop meat in 4 batches using on/off turns until finely ground.   Place in a large bowl. Place eggs in workbowl and whirl just until mixed. Add to meat. Add remaining ingredients and toss together. Set aside.

SAUCE

1 large carrot
1 large stalk of celery } cut in 1-1/2" lengths
1 medium onion
1/2 cup water
1-1/2 cup tomato sauce
1/3 cup brown sugar
1/4 cup maple syrup
1/4 cup raisins
2 chunks sour salt
salt, garlic powder, onion powder to taste

Insert steel blade. Place vegetables in workbowl and process turning on/off until finely chopped. Put vegetables in 5 quart Dutch oven with water and bring to a simmer. Add remaining ingredients. Heat sauce to simmering point. Roll meat into 1-1/2" balls and place in sauce. As you complete a layer, turn cooked side up and continue adding meatballs. Cover and simmer 45-60 minutes. If sauce dries out, add 1/4 cup water until desired consistency is achieved.

Shredded Beef and Vegetables

*1 lb. flank steak or other lean beef, partially frozen and cut
    to fit feed tube*
2 medium onions, halved
2 large green peppers, quartered lengthwise
1/2 cup peanut or salad oil

MARINADE

> *2 tbs. soy sauce*
> *1 tsp. sugar*
> *1 tbs. cornstarch*
> *1 tbs. oil*

SEASONING SAUCE

> *1 tsp. sugar*
> *1 tsp. cornstarch*
> *1 tbs. water*
> *2 tbs. soy sauce*

Remove meat from freezer about 45 minutes before slicing. It should still be quite firm.

Insert slicing disk and slice meat. (If meat slices are wide enough to fill feed tube you may take the slices, stack them and wedge them, sliced side down in the bottom of the feed tube). Replace the cover, exert firm pressure and slice again. You will get matchstick slices of meat. Remove meat and set aside. Wedge peppers and onions in feed tube and slice using medium pressure.

Combine marinade ingredients and toss with meat. Let stand 15 minutes.

Heat half the oil and stir-fry meat. Remove meat. Add remaining oil and stir-fry vegetables. Add beef and seasoning sauce and heat through. Serve with rice.

*Try the Cuisinarts® fine slicing disk or the French fry disk to cut meat.

Burgundy Pecan Burgers

1 lb. beef in 1" cubes
1 tsp. salt
1/4 tsp. pepper
1/2 cup pecans
1/3 cup Burgundy

Insert steel blade. Place 1/2 lb. beef, 1/2 tsp. salt, 1/8 tsp. pepper in workbowl and chop using on/off turns until desired degree of fineness is achieved. Add 1/2 of nuts after 3 turns. Repeat with remaining meat and nuts.

Form into patties. Brown on both sides. Add Burgundy, cover and simmer 5 minutes.

Makes 4.

Stuffed Beef Tenderloin

3 lb. beef tenderloin
3 pieces stale white bread
1 medium onion, quartered
1 rib celery, cut in 1-1/2" pieces
1 sprig parsley
1/4 lb. mushrooms
5 tbs. butter
3/4 tsp. salt
1/8 tsp. pepper
1/2 tsp. basil
4 slices bacon

Insert steel blade. Break bread up. Place bread in workbowl with parsley and process until coarse crumbs form. Place in mixing bowl. Add celery and onion to workbowl and chop with 3-4 on/off turns. **Insert slicing disk.** Fill feed tube with mushrooms and slice. Saute mushrooms, onions and celery until onion is soft. Toss mixture with crumbs. Season with salt, pepper and basil.

Make a lengthwise cut, three-fourths of the way through the meat. Fill lightly with stuffing and close with toothpicks. Place bacon diagonally across the top, covering the picks and pocket. Place in 9" x 13" baking dish and bake uncovered at 350° for 1 hour, for medium rare.

Serves 6.

Burgundy Meatballs

2 lb. chuck, cut in 1-1/2" cubes
2 slices of stale bread
.1/3 cup water
2 tsp. salt

SAUCE

1 large carrot, cut in 1-1/2" pieces
1 large rib celery, cut in 1-1/2" pieces
1 medium onion, quartered
1/4 lb. fresh mushrooms
2   13-3/4 oz. cans beef broth (reserve 1/2 cup liquid)
1/2 cup Burgundy
1/2 of 6 oz. can of tomato paste
3 tbs. cornstarch
1   9 oz. package frozen artichoke hearts defrosted
1 tsp. sugar
1/2 cup cold water

Insert steel blade. Process bread to fine crumbs using on/off method, then allow machine to run. Set aside. **Replace steel blade** and process meat in 4 batches, using on/off turns until desired fineness is reached. Combine with salt, water and bread crumbs.

Insert slicing blade. Slice mushrooms and set aside. **Insert steel blade** and place vegetables in bowl. Chop finely, using 4-5 on/off turns. Place in large saucepan and add broth (reserve 1/2 cup) and tomato paste. Heat to simmering. Roll meatballs to desired size and place gently in simmering liquid. Add Burgundy, cover and cook on low heat 30-40 minutes, or until meatballs are cooked through. Add mushrooms and artichoke hearts and cook 10 minutes more on medium heat uncovered. Mix cornstarch and sugar and add to reserved broth. Mix well and pour slowly into saucepan. Stir and cook uncovered mixing frequently, until sauce thickens.

Serves 4-6.

Carbonnades of Beef Flamande

2 tbs. butter
1-1/2 lb. onions peeled
1/2 lb. mushrooms, cleaned
1 clove garlic
3 lb. round steak or chuck, cut in 1" cubes
salt and pepper
1/4 lb. bacon
3 tbs. flour
2 cups light beer
1 cup beef broth
1 tbs. wine vinegar
2 tsp. brown sugar
1/2 tsp. thyme
1 leek, trimmed and washed
3 sprigs parsley
1 bay leaf

Optional: 1 bag of baby carrots, cleaned and cooked.

Insert steel blade. Slice mushrooms in batches using medium pressure. Set aside. Place onions in feed tube and slice (on their sides if possible. If not, halve and stand vertically and slice with firm pressure). Wipe bowl. Turn machine on, drop in garlic and mince. Set aside.

Sprinkle meat with salt and pepper. Fry bacon in Dutch oven. Set bacon aside. Add butter to pan and brown beef. Remove from pan. Cook onions in drippings stirring until brown. Add mushrooms and cook 3-4 minutes. Add flour and cook, stirring over low heat until flour begins to brown. Gradually add beer and broth stirring and scraping pan with a whisk. When thickened and smooth add vinegar, sugar and garlic and return to a boil. Return meat to Dutch oven. Tie leek, parsley and bay leaf together in cheesecloth and add to casserole. Sprinkle thyme over and mix well. Season with salt and pepper. Cover and bake 1 - 1-1/2 hours at 350°. Add water if sauce dries up too much. Add cooked carrots during last 1/2 hour of cooking time.

Paupiettes de Veau

12 veal scallops
1 tsp. salt
1/4 tsp. pepper
2 tbs. butter or margarine
2 carrots, cut into 2" lengths
1 onion, halved
1 clove garlic

STUFFING
2 medium onions
1 cup walnuts
1/2 cup parsley leaves
2 pieces stale bread
4 tbs. margarine
1-1/2 tsp. thyme
1 tsp. tarragon
1/2 tsp. salt
1/4 tsp. pepper

MADIERA SAUCE
2 tbs. flour
2 tbs. butter
2 cups chicken broth
1 cup Madiera
1/2 tsp. pepper
gravy seasoning

Insert slicing disk. Wedge carrot pieces in feed tube and slice. Slice onion. Place in bottom of casserole. **Insert steel blade** and mince garlic. Sprinkle over vegetables.

Pound veal into 4" x 6" pieces, sprinkle with salt and pepper.

To prepare stuffing. **Insert steel blade** and process bread crumbs. Set aside. Chop nuts with 4-5 on/off turns. Set aside. Mince parsley. Set aside. Chop onions with 3-4 on/off turns and set aside. Wipe bowl.

Melt butter in a skillet, add onions, nuts, parsley, thyme, tarragon, salt and pepper. Cook 5 minutes or until onions are tender. Remove from heat, add bread crumbs and toss lightly. Loosely place 3 tbs. stuffing in the center of each piece of veal. Roll and secure with toothpicks. Heat 2 tbs. margarine until hot, add veal rolls and brown quickly. Place veal in casserole over sliced vegetables. Reserve drippings.

Add 2 tbs. margarine to drippings in the skillet. Add 2 tbs. flour, cook and stir until brown, 3-5 minutes. Remove from heat, add broth, Madiera and pepper. Slowly add a few drops of gravy seasoning. Cook 3 minutes until thickened. Pour over veal and vegetables. Cover and bake 30-35 minutes at 350°. Baste occasionally.

Serve 4-6.

Veal Chasseur

1-1/2 lb. veal cutlets
4 tbs. butter
1/2 cup dry white wine
1 large onion, quartered
1 lb. mushrooms, sliced
1/2 cup parsley leaves
1 tsp. salt
dash pepper
1 small lemon

BROWN SAUCE

1 large onion
1 large carrot
1 clove garlic
1 rib celery
4 tbs. butter
2 tbs. cornstarch
3 cups beef boullion
2 tbs. Madiera
1/2 tsp. thyme
1 bay leaf
1/2 tsp. salt
6 peppercorns

Prepare Brown Sauce: Cut vegetables in 1-1/2" pieces and place in workbowl **with steel blade.** Turn on/off until a coarse chop is achieved. Heat butter in large skillet and saute vegetables until golden. Add cornstarch to 1/2 of boullion. Pour in skillet. Add remaining ingredients. Bring to a boil and reduce heat. Cover and simmer 30 minutes, stirring occasionally, until reduced to 2 cups. Strain liquid. **Insert steel blade** and puree vegetables. Add to sauce. (Remember to remove bay leaf and peppercorns.)

Cut veal into 1-1/4" pieces or pound until thin. Saute in butter 10 minutes. Add 1/4 cup of the wine to help remove sticky pieces from skillet. Remove from pan and keep warm. Saute onions and mushrooms in remaining juices. Add remaining wine and simmer several minutes. Return veal to pan, stir in brown sauce and parsley. Season to taste with salt and pepper. Garnish with lemon slices and parsley.

To make lemon slices: Cut top and bottom off small lemon. Wedge in feed tube. **With slicing blade in place** exert medium pressure.

Serves 3-4.

Veal Sausage Patties

2 lb. lean veal shoulder, cut in 1" cubes
2 tsp. salt
1 tsp. sugar
1-1/2 tsp. rosemary
1/2 tsp. ground coriander
1 tsp. prepared mustard
1/2 tsp. ground sage
1/8 tsp. black pepper
1/8 tsp. cayenne
1/4 tsp. nutmeg
1/2 cup crushed ice

Insert steel blade. Add spices to workbowl and whirl until combined. Set aside.

Reinsert steel blade. Add 1/2 lb. of meat to workbowl and sprinkle with 1/4 of the seasonings. Process, turning on/off until finely ground. Remove from bowl. Repeat three more times, each time with 1/2 lb. of meat.

When all meat is processed toss lightly with 1/2 cup crushed ice. Gently shape into 16 patties. Wrap and freeze if desired. Broil or barbeque 2 minutes on each side.

Beef and Eggplant Pie

1   9" baked pastry shell
1 small eggplant, peeled and quartered lengthwise
4 tbs. margarine
1 medium onion
3 sprigs parsley
3 celery tops
1 clove garlic
3/4 lb. beef chuck, in 1-1/2" cubes
1 tsp. salt
1/8 tsp. pepper
1/8 tsp. nutmeg
1/4 tsp. cinnamon
1   8 oz. can tomato sauce

Preheat oven to 350°.

Insert slicing disk. Slice eggplant and saute slices in margarine. **Insert steel blade.** Mince parsley, onion and celery tops with 4-5 on/off turns. Set aside. Process meat with on/off turns until finely ground. Combine all ingredients but tomato sauce. Mound in pie shell. Pour tomato sauce over the top and bake 45-60 minutes.

Serves 4-6.

Fruited Lamb Curry

1 cup dried apples
1/2 cup dried pitted prunes
1/2 cup raisins
1-1/2 cup water
1-1/2 cup boneless lamb shoulder, cubed
1 tsp. salt
2 tbs. oil
2 medium onions, quartered
1/4 cup salted peanuts
2 medium bananas (firm)*
2 tbs. curry powder
2 tbs. wine vinegar
1 tbs. lemon juice

Soak fruit in water for 1 hour, turning several times.

Insert steel blade. Chop peanuts with 2-3 on/off turns. Set aside. Chop onions with 3-4 on/off turns.

Heat oil in Dutch oven and brown meat. Sprinkle on salt at end of cooking. Set meat aside and pour off all but 2 tbs. oil. Add onions and cook until soft. Add curry powder and blend well. Add meat, fruits and liquid, vinegar and lemon juice. Bring to a boil. Reduce heat. Simmer, covered, 1 hour or until meat is tender. Stir occasionally and add small amounts of water to pan.

At serving time mound meat on a platter and sprinkle with chopped peanuts. Surround with sliced bananas. Serve with rice.

*Slice bananas at the last moment. Cut bananas in half and wedge halves into feed tube. Slice with firm pressure.

Hawaiian Chicken

2 2-3 pound chickens, cut in eighths
2 celery ribs, cut in 1-1/2" lengths
1 green pepper, cut in 1-1/2" pieces
1-1/2 medium onions quartered
1 - 20 oz. can pineapple chunks, drained
salt, pepper, oregano, paprika

SAUCE

    1/2 cup orange marmalade
    1/4 cup vinegar
    1/4 cup ketchup
    3 tbs. pineapple juice (syrup from can)

Insert steel blade. Place half of cut up vegetables in workbowl and process using on/off turns until finely chopped. Remove and set aside. Repeat with remaining vegetables.

Season chicken pieces with spices and place in one layer in large casserole. Spread chopped vegetables over chicken and cover tightly with cover or heavy foil. Bake at 400° for 1 hour, turning once.

Combine sauce ingredients in workbowl **with plastic blade** and combine. Arrange pineapple on chicken and pour sauce over. Cover again and bake 1/2 hour covered, and 1/2 hour uncovered. If sauce begins to dry up add additional pineapple syrup.

Serves 6-8.

Zucchini Chicken

1 broiler, fryer chicken, quartered
3 medium tomatoes, peeled, quartered
2 green peppers, cut in 1-1/2" pieces
2 medium zucchini, cut in 1-1/2" lengths
1 small onion, halved
11 tbs. olive oil
bouquet garni
salt

Insert steel bade. Separately chop each vegetable using 3-4 chops for each (coarse chop). Set aside.

Brown chicken in 3 tbs. oil. Remove chicken. Add additional 1/2 cup oil and heat. Add vegetables and fry briefly, stirring constantly. Add chicken, bouquet garni and simmer, covered, until chicken is done, about 30 minutes. Remove bouquet garni. Season with salt. Thicken with flour and water paste if desired.

Serves 4.

Chicken Tonnato

3-1/2 lb. (broiler) cut up*
1 onion
2 ribs celery, cut in 1-1/2" pieces
2 peeled carrots
1 tsp. salt
2 qts. water
1 cup mayonnaise
1   3 oz. can tuna, drained
2 anchovies
1 tbs. lemon juice
salt and pepper to taste
1 head iceberg lettuce
1/3 cup capers
2 ripe tomatoes, in wedges
parsley

Place chicken in Dutch oven with onion, celery, carrots and salt and water. Bring to a boil. Cover and boil gently for 1 hour or until chicken is tender. Drain (save broth for a later use). Cool chicken. Remove and discard skin. Set chicken aside.

Insert steel blade. Chop celery with 4-5 on/off turns, or until finely minced. **Remove steel blade. Insert plastic blade.** Add mayonnaise, tuna, anchovies and lemon juice to workbowl. Process until smooth. Add salt and pepper to taste. Set aside. Clean bowl.

Insert slicing disk. Cut lettuce into small wedges and shred using firm pressure.

Place lettuce on serving platter. Arrange chicken on lettuce. Spoon sauce over chicken. Garnish with parsley, tomatoes and capers. Chill.

Serve cold.

*Leftover turkey, chicken or turkey roll may be substituted.

Chicken Breasts in Phyllo Dough

1/4 lb. butter
1 onion
1/2 lb. mushrooms
2 tbs. minced parsley
1 clove garlic
1-1/2 tbs. flour
1/3 cup vermouth
salt and pepper to taste
2 tbs. oil
4 boned chicken breast halves
8 phyllo leaves
1/3 cup melted butter
bread crumbs

Insert steel blade. Mince parsley and set aside. Peel and quarter onion, place in bowl and chop with 3-4 quick turns. Set aside. Place 1/2 of mushrooms in workbowl and chop using 3-4 quick turns, checking after each turn to see that the mushrooms are not too fine. Repeat with rest of mushrooms.

In skillet, heat 3 tbs. butter and saute onion until golden. Set aside. Heat 3 more tbs. butter and saute mushrooms until juices evaporate, then add onions, parsley, and garlic and saute a little more. Stir in flour, mixing well, and add vermouth. Stir over medium heat until thickened. Season with salt and pepper. Set aside.

In skillet, heat remaining butter and oil and saute breasts one minute on each side. Wrap one breast in two phyllo leaves, keeping unused sheets between waxed paper and a damp towel. Butter one sheet of phyllo and sprinkle with crumbs. Cover with second sheet of phyllo and butter again. Place chicken on leaves (about 4" from the end of the short side) and put 1/4 of mushroom mixture on top and roll it up like a blintz, tucking in corners. Butter outside well and bake open side down at 350° for 35 minutes or until done.

Five Spice Baked Chicken

2-1/2 - 3 lb. whole broiler-fryer
oil
1 tsp. five spice powder
2 tbs. soy sauce
2 tbs. dry sherry
1 tbs. cornstarch

Preheat oven to 375°.

Rinse chicken and pat dry. Sprinkle cavity with salt. Brush with oil. Sprinkle with Five Spice Powder. Place chicken, breast side up on rack in shallow roasting pan. Roast uncovered 1-1/4 - 1-1/2 hours, basting with mixture of soy sauce and sherry during last 15 minutes. Place chicken on serving platter and keep warm. Measure pan drippings, skim off excess fat. Add enough water to make 1 cup. Blend in cornstarch. Cook and stir until mixture is thickened and bubbly. Serve with chicken and Oriental stir-fried vegetables.

FIVE SPICE POWDER

2 tbs. whole peppercorns
2 tbs. fennel seed
36 whole cloves
12 whole star anise
12" stick cinnamon, broken up

Insert steel blade. Place ingredients in workbowl. Process until a fine powder forms. Store tightly covered. Makes 1/2 cup. Can be used in other Oriental recipes.

Arroz Con Pollo

1/2 tsp. paprika
2   2-1/2-3 lb. chickens, cut up
      or 8 breast halves
2 medium onions, quartered
2 green peppers, cut in 1-1/2" pieces
2 cloves garlic
1-1/4 tsp. salt
1/2 tsp. pepper
1/4 cup olive oil
2 cups water
1   28 oz. can tomatoes
2 chicken boullion cubes
1/4 tsp. saffron
1 bay leaf
1/2 tsp. oregano
2 cups raw rice
1   10 oz. package frozen peas, defrosted
1 can artichoke hearts
pimento strips

Preheat oven to 350°.

Season chicken with 1 tsp. salt, pepper and paprika. Heat oil in large skillet, add chicken pieces and brown on all sides. Place in 9" x 13" x 2" oven casserole.

Insert steel blade. Place onions and garlic in workbowl and chop coarsely, using 2-3 on/off turns. Empty workbowl into skillet. Repeat with green pepper. Saute onion, pepper and garlic until tender. Take tomatoes out of liquid and place in workbowl **with steel blade.** Chop coarsely using 2 on/off turns. Add water, tomatoes and liquid, boullion cubes, seasonings and 1/4 tsp. of the salt. Bring to a boil.

Pour rice into casserole between the chicken pieces. Pour boiling liquid over chicken and rice. Cover tightly and bake 45 minutes. Uncover and toss peas into rice. Arrange artichokes and pimento strips on top, cover and cook 10 minutes longer or until most of liquid is absorbed.

Party Chicken Salad

3 large chicken breast halves, cooked, boned and
    partially frozen (2 cups sliced)
2 tbs. lemon juice
1/2 tsp. salt
2 large ribs celery, cut in 2" lengths
1 cup seedless grapes
2 hardboiled eggs, chilled and halved
1/2 cup mayonnaise
1/4 cup toasted almonds

Insert slicing disk. Slice points off chicken breasts. Cut chicken into wedges that will fit into feed tube, wedge in tightly, exert firm pressure and slice. (You will have a combination of slices and shreds.) If you prefer, cube the chicken by hand. Sprinkle lemon juice and salt over chicken and chill several hours.

Insert plastic blade. Chop eggs coarsely using 3 on/off turns. Place in a bowl and set aside.

Insert slicing disk. Wedge celery in and slice using medium pressure. Place grapes in feed tube and slice using medium pressure. Add celery and grapes to bowl.

When chicken has been chilled, add celery, grapes, eggs, toasted almonds and mayonnaise. Toss lightly.

Garnish with daisy trim*.

*DAISY TRIM — Quarter two hardboiled eggs lengthwise. Remove yolks. Arrange whites for petals in center of mound. Sieve yolks over top of whites.

Chicken Kiev

1 cup butter
1/4 cup parsley leaves
1 clove garlic
3 eggs
3/4 tsp. salt
1/4 tsp. pepper
flour
1-1/2 cup dry bread crumbs
6 whole chicken breasts, skinned, boned and flattened
salad oil

Insert steel blade. Place garlic and parsley in workbowl and chop finely. Cut butter into 8 pieces and place on blades. Add salt and pepper. Process only until contents have been combined. Form seasoned butter into a 6" square on a sheet of foil or waxed paper. Freeze until firm, about 1/2 hour.

Cut breasts in half, wash and pat dry. Cut butter into 12 oblong pieces, placing a pat on each piece of chicken. Fold the chicken around the butter, making sure to enclose butter completely.

Insert plastic blade. Beat eggs and pour into shallow dish. Coat each piece of chicken with flour, then dip into the egg and coat with bread crumbs. Shape breasts into triangles, tucking edges inside. Cover and refrigerate one hour. Heat oil to 360° several inches deep in large skillet or Dutch oven. Fry until brown, about 8-10 minutes, turning gently with tongs. Drain on paper towel. Keep warm in oven or serve immediately.

Chicken Cacciatora

1 - 3 lb. broiler, cut up
1/4 cup olive oil
2 medium onions
2 cloves garlic
1 lb. can tomatoes
1 - 8 oz. can tomato sauce
1/2 tsp. celery seed
1/4 tsp. pepper
1 bay leaf
1/4 cup sauterne

Insert slicing disk. Slice top and bottom off onions, wedge into feed tube sideways and slice. Set aside. **Insert steel blade.** Turn machine on and drop garlic in. When garlic is minced remove and add to onions. Pour remaining ingredients except bay leaf and sauterne into workbowl. Turn on/off twice.

Heat oil in Dutch oven, brown chicken slowly. Set aside. Add onions and garlic and cook until tender. Return chicken to skillet. Add bay leaf, pour sauce over and cover and simmer 45 minutes. Add wine; cook uncovered about 20 minutes or until chicken is tender and sauce has thickened.

Serves 3-4.

Lo Mein

1/2 lb. vermicelli cooked and drained
2 cups cooked beef, chicken or seafood partially frozen
1/3 of a small head of green cabbage
1 can water chestnuts
1 bunch scallions, cut in thirds
1 large onion
6 mushrooms
1/2 cup chicken broth
1/4 cup soy sauce
2 tbs. cornstarch
2 tsp. sugar
1/2 tsp. sesame oil
1/4-1/2 cup peanut or salad oil
1 can bean sprouts

Insert slicing disk. Wedge meat or chicken into feed tube and slice, using firm pressure. Set aside. Wedge cabbage into feed tube and slice. Set aside. Cut onion in half, wedge pieces in and slice. Wedge scallions in feed tube and slice.

Heat 1/4 cup oil in wok and stir-fry onions, cabbage, and scallions. Add chicken and stir-fry. Remove from wok. Add remaining oil to wok.

While chicken and vegetables are cooking, pour mushrooms into feed tube and slice, using firm pressure. Repeat with water chestnuts. Add mushrooms and water chestnuts to wok and continue to stir-fry until mushrooms are cooked. Add cooked noodles and toss with vegetables. Combine seasonings and pour over noodles. Cook and stir until heated through and sauce has thickened.

Serves 4.

Italian Quiche

2 medium zucchini, cut in thirds
2 medium onions, cut in half
4 oz. mozzarella cheese
3 tbs. olive oil
15 oz. ricotta cheese
1 cup milk
3 eggs
1 tsp. salt

TOMATO SAUCE
1 clove garlic
1/3 cup parsley leaves
1 lb. can whole tomatoes
1 - 8 oz. can tomato sauce
1/2 tsp. oregano
dash of pepper
1/2 tsp. salt

PASTRY SHELL
10" pastry shell prebaked for 10
  minutes, at 350°. Use technique
  described on page 121 for "One Shell
  Pie Crust"
2 cups flour
1 tsp. salt
3/4 cup shortening
1/4 cup ice water

Insert slicing disk, slice mozzarella cheese. Set aside. Slice zucchini and onions. **Insert plastic blade,** combine ricotta, eggs, milk and 1 teaspoon salt. Set aside. Wash bowl.

In a large skillet heat 2 tbs. oil and saute zucchini and onions. Squeeze out excess liquid from cooked vegetables in a paper towel.

Insert steel blade. Place parsley and garlic in workbowl and mince. Place in skillet with 1 tbs. heated oil and saute, stirring constantly for one minute. Place remaining sauce ingredients in workbowl and turn on/off twice to mash. Add tomato mixture to skillet and cook, stirring occasionally about 15 minutes or until liquid is reduced to about 2 cups.

Spread cooked vegetables over prebaked shell and spread 1/2 cup tomato sauce over. Pour cheese mixture over. Bake at 375° for 40 minutes or until set in center. Arrange cheese slices on top of pie, spoon some of the sauce between slices. Bake 5-7 minutes more. Garnish with parsley and olives. Serve with remaining tomato sauce.

Gert's Chicken Chow Mein

3 large chicken breast halves, cooked and boned, partially frozen.
2 medium onions, halved
3 ribs celery, cut in 2" lengths
3/4 cup water
1 can drained bean sprouts
1/4 cup oil
2 tbs. cornstarch ⎫
2 tbs. soy sauce ⎬   combined
1 tsp. sugar ⎪
1/2 cup water ⎭

    Insert slicing disk. Wedge onions in feed tube and slice. Set aside. Repeat with celery. Wedge large pieces of chicken in feed tube and slice.

    Heat oil in large skillet, saute onion until soft. Add chicken and saute 5 minutes more. Add celery and 3/4 cup water and saute until celery is soft. Add bean sprouts and soy mixture. Cover and simmer until sauce is thickened and glazed (3-5 minutes). Season with salt and pepper.

Serves 4.

Chinese Omelet

3/4 cup cooked chicken, pork or shrimp
2 scallions, cut in 2" pieces
1 tbs. cornstarch
1 cup chicken broth
1-1/2 tbs. soy sauce
1 tsp. sugar
2 eggs
1/2 tsp. salt
2 tbs. water
2 tbs. oil

    Insert steel blade. Mince chicken and scallions with 3-4 on/off turns. Set aside.

    Mix cornstarch with the broth, soy sauce and sugar. Cook over low heat, stirring constantly until thickened. Keep warm while preparing omelets.

    Insert plastic blade. Place eggs, salt and water in workbowl and turn on/off twice. Add meat and scallions and turn on/off to combine.

    Heat oil in two 6" skillets until it bubbles. Divide the mixture between the two pans and fry until browned on both sides. Place in serving dish and pour sauce over the top.

    Serves 2.

Lo Cal-Marinated
Tuna and Vegetables

2 large carrots, cut in 2" lengths
1/2 small head cauliflower, broken into florets (1-1/2 cups)
1 - 10 oz. package frozen peas
2 ribs celery, cut in 2" lengths
2 scallions, cut in 2" lengths
1 6-1/2-7 oz. can tuna, drained and flaked
3/4 cup Tomato Salad Dressing

Insert slicing disk. Lay carrot pieces horizontally in feed tube. Exert firm pressure and slice. Remove carrots and stack slices in order (if possible). Move the pusher up about 2" and replace a stack of carrots in the bottom of the feed tube, sliced side down. Wedge the pieces firmly, then replace cover and slice. You will have julienne slices.

Cook carrots and cauliflower together in boiling salted water for 10 minutes. Add peas, cook 5 minutes more or until vegetables are tender crisp.

While vegetables are cooking, **insert slicing disk.** Wedge celery and scallions in feed tube together and slice.

Place cooked, drained vegetables, celery, scallions and tuna. Toss with dressing. Serve on lettuce.

225 calories per serving. Serves 3.

Tomato Salad Dressing

1-8 oz. can tomato sauce
2 tbs. tarragon vinegar
1 tsp. worcestershire sauce
1/2 tsp. salt
1/2 tsp. dill weed
1/2 tsp. dried basil
1/2 tsp. onion juice

Insert plastic blade. Combine ingredients in workbowl and whirl.

Pancake Souffle
With Sauteed Apples

2 large eggs
1/2 cup milk
1/2 cup flour
1/2 tsp. sugar
1/4 tsp. salt

Preheat oven to 425°.

Place 1 tablespoon butter or margarine in 10″ cast iron skillet or pie plate and put in oven to melt. **Insert steel blade.** Put milk, salt, flour and sugar in workbowl. Process quickly, using on/off method until smooth, scraping down the sides if necessary. With machine off, add eggs and turn on/off several times until mixture is just blended, not beaten.

Remove skillet from oven and swirl butter around bottom and sides of pan. Pour batter in skillet and return to oven. Bake 15-20 minutes or until crisp, puffed and brown. Serve immediately with preserves, cinnamon and sugar or sauteed apples.

APPLES
3-4 tart apples
3 tbs. butter
1/8 tsp. nutmeg
1/4 tsp. cinnamon
1/3 cup sugar

Insert plastic blade. Combine sugar, cinnamon and nutmeg in bowl. Turn on/off to combine. Remove from bowl and set aside.

Peel, core and halve apples. **With slicing blade,** stack apple halves vertically in feed tube and slice, exerting firm pressure. Melt butter in skillet, place apples in pan and saute for 5 minutes. Pour in reserved sugar mixture, cover and cook 10 minutes more.

Makes enough to accompany 2-3 pancake souffles.

Sylvia's French Toast

8 slices white bread
1 cup jelly, any flavor
4 eggs, separated
1/2 tsp. cream of tartar
1/2 cup milk
2 tbs. sugar
1 tbs. flour
oil for deep frying

Remove crusts from bread. Make four jelly sandwiches, using 1/4 cup jelly on each. Remove crusts. Cut sandwiches into 4 triangles.

Separate eggs. **Insert steel blade** in the clean, dry workbowl. Add egg whites and 1/2 tsp. cream of tartar. Beat until stiff. Place in mixing bowl.

Insert plastic blade. Add yolk, milk, sugar and flour to workbowl and mix. Fold yolks into whites and blend without losing volume.

Heat oil for deep frying 370°. Dip each sandwich piece into batter. Fry each piece on both sides. Drain on paper towels and serve immediately.

Makes 16 pieces. Serves 3-4.

Salmon Noodle Bake

8 oz. macaroni, cooked
1 1 lb. can salmon, flaked
1/2 lb. cheddar cheese
1 rib celery, cut in 1-1/2" lengths
1 small onion
3 tbs. butter
3 tbs. flour
2-1/2 cups milk
1 tsp. worcestershire sauce
1 tsp. dry mustard

Preheat oven to 350°

Insert shredding disk. Cut cheese to fit feed tube and shred. Set aside. **Insert steel blade.** Chop celery and onion with 3-4 on/off turns. Saute in butter until soft. Stir in flour and mustard. Add milk and cook until thickened. Add 1-1/2 cups cheese and stir until melted.

Combine salmon, macaroni and cheese sauce. Pour into greased 2-1/2-3 qt. casserole. Sprinkle with remaining cheeses. Bake 35 minutes or until bubbling.

Cold Salmon Mousse

1 envelope unflavored gelatin
2 tbs. lemon juice
1 large onion, quartered
1/2 cup boiling water
1/2 cup mayonnaise
1/4 tsp. paprika
1 tbs. dill, fresh
1 - 1 lb. can salmon, drained, boned and chunked
1 cup sour cream

Soften gelatin in lemon juice. **Insert steel blade.** Mince dill and set aside. Add gelatin mixture, boiling water and onion to workbowl. Process until smooth. Add mayonnaise, paprika, dill and salmon and process until just blended. **Insert plastic blade** and add sour cream and process, using on/off turns until sour cream is combined and mixture is smooth. Pour into oiled 4 cup mold and chill 4 hours or overnight.

Unmold on plate and garnish with fresh dill sprigs and cherry tomatoes.

Serve with Cucumber-Dill Sauce.

Cucumber Dill Sauce
(For Cold Salmon Mousse)

1 cucumber, peeled, seeded, cut in half
salt
1 cup sour cream
1 tbs. lemon juice
1 tsp. dill weed
1 tsp. chopped chives
1/4 tsp. white pepper

Insert grating disk. Shred cucumber. Place in mixing bowl. Sprinkle with salt. Let stand 1 hour. Drain thoroughly. Combine with remaining ingredients and chill.

Bacon and Cheese Souflee

1/4 lb. cheddar cheese, cut in 1" cubes
2 tbs. butter
2 tbs. flour
3/4 cup hot milk
4 egg yolks
1/8 tsp. salt
1/8 tsp. dry mustard
6 egg whites
3 strips cooked, crumbled bacon
pinch cayenne

Preheat oven to 375°. Grease a 1-1/2 qt. souflee dish.

Insert steel blade. Grate cheese until fine. Add butter and flour and process several seconds. With machine running, add hot milk through the feed tube and process until smooth.

Cook cheese mixture in top part of a double boiler. Add egg yolks one at a time, whisking after each addition. Season with salt, cayenne and mustard.

Wash and dry bowl and blade thoroughly. **Insert steel blade.** Add egg whites and process until stiff peaks form. Fold whites and bacon into cooled cheese sauce. Pour into prepared souflee dish. Bake 17-20 minutes. Serve at once.

*You may want to use your electric mixer for the egg whites to get better volume.

Broccoli Crepes

BASIC CREPES
3 eggs
1 cup milk
1 cup sifted flour*
1/4 tsp. salt
2 tbs. melted butter

Insert steel blade. Place eggs, flour and salt in workbowl. Whirl until smooth. Add milk and melted butter and whirl 15 seconds. Let batter rest, covered in the refrigerator 1 hour or overnight.

Prepare crepes by pouring into a traditional crepe pan or using the newer dipping method.

*If you use Gold Medal's Wondra Instant Flour, you do not have to let the batter rest. Stir the bubbles out and use immediately.

BROCCOLI FILLING
1 small head broccoli (20 ounces, uncooked)
1 small onion, halved
1-1/2 cups mushrooms
1 - 5 oz. can water chestnuts
3 tbs. butter or margarine
2 tbs. flour
1/2 cup light cream
1/4 cup chicken broth
1 tsp. salt
1/8 tsp. pepper
2 tbs. parmesan cheese (cut up a 6 ounce piece into
       1/2" pieces. Process all at once. Remove 2 tbs. for
       filling, save remainder for sauce)

Cut florets off broccoli, clean and cut up stems and boil or steam all parts until tender. Drain and set aside.

Insert steel blade. Place mushrooms in workbowl and chop, using 2 on/off turns. Place in large skillet with 3 tbs. butter. Place onion in workbowl and chop, using 3 on/off turns. Add to skillet. Saute mushrooms and onions. **Reinsert steel blade.** Chop water chestnuts with 3-4 on/off turns. Set aside. Add broccoli to workbowl and chop using 3-4 on/off turns.

Stir flour into skillet. Add cream and chicken broth. Cook stirring until thickened. Add 2 tbs. grated parmesan cheese, water chestnuts, salt, pepper and broccoli. Combine well. Set aside.

Prepare Sauce.

CHEESE SAUCE

1/2 cup butter or margarine
1/2 cup flour
1-1/2 cups light cream
2 cups milk
1-1/2 cups grated parmesan cheese
2 tsp. prepared mustard
1 tsp. salt

In large saucepan melt butter and stir in flour. Add cream and milk and stir until well blended. Add cheese, mustard and salt. Stir until thickened and cheese has melted.

Divide filling among crepes and roll up. Place in a single layer in a greased shallow casserole. Pour sauce over the top of the crepes. Bake uncovered in a 350° oven for 25-30 minutes or until bubbly and light brown.

Makes 16 filled crepes.

Chinese Seafood Rice Casserole

2 cups cooked rice
1/2 medium pepper
2 stalks celery, cut into 1-1/2" chunks
1 medium onion
1 can water chestnuts
1/4 lb. cheddar cheese
1 - 6-1/2 oz. can crab meat
2 - 4-1/2 oz. can shrimp
1 cup mayonnaise
1 cup tomato juice
1/2 cup toasted slivered almonds
paprika

Insert steel blade. Chop pepper and onion together using 2-3 on/off turns. Set aside. Repeat with celery.

Insert shredding disk. Shred cheese with firm pressure. Set aside.

Insert slicing disk. Pour drained water chestnuts into feed tube and slice.

Combine all ingredients but cheese, almonds and paprika. Pour into a greased 2-1/2 qt. casserole and top with reserved ingredients. Bake at 350° for 25 minutes.

Flounder Dlugere

1-1/2 lb. flounder or sole fillets
4 tomatoes, peeled and quartered
1 tbs. butter
salt and pepper
1/4 cup dry white wine
SAUCE

   5 tbs. butter
   1 small onion, halved
   3 mushrooms
   6 tbs. flour
   1 cup milk
   1/2 cup chicken broth
   1/2 cup heavy cream
   1 tsp. salt
   1 tbs. Cognac
   1/2 tbs. white pepper
   1/4 tsp. dry mustard

   Preheat oven to 400°.

Insert steel blade and chop tomatoes with 2 on/off turns. Cook in 1 tbs. butter until soft. Place fillets in baking dish and cover with tomatoes and wine. Season with salt and pepper. Cover and bake 20 minutes. While fish is cooking, prepare sauce.

SAUCE

Insert steel blade and chop mushrooms with 2 on/off turns. Set aside. Chop onion with 2 on/off turns. Place mushrooms and onions in medium saucepan and saute in 2 tbs. butter for 2 minutes. Add remaining 3 tbs. butter and melt. Blend in flour and stir well. Remove from heat and add broth, milk and cream, a little at a time, stirring constantly. Season with mustard, salt, pepper and cognac. Return to heat and cook until thickened. Cook 2-3 minutes more.

Drain liquid from fish casserole. Pour sauce over fish and tomatoes. Heat 20 minutes in oven at 350°.

Charlie's Favorite Pizza

1/2 cup parsley leaves
4 scallions, white parts
2 pimentos
1/2 cup mayonnaise
1 tbs. lemon juice
1 large, firm tomato, sliced lengthwise
2 cans (6-3/4 oz.) tuna, drained and chunked
1/2 lb. Swiss or American cheese, presliced
1 can refrigerated crescent rolls

Separate rolls and press into 12" pizza pan. Seal perforations and form crust with 1/2" rim. Bake at 375° for 15 minutes. Remove from oven.

Insert steel blade. Chop scallions and parsley. Set aside. Chop pimento. **Insert plastic blade.** Add tuna, mayonnaise, parsley, scallions and lemon juice. Turn on/off, scraping down sides until just combined.

Arrange cheese over crust. Spread tuna over entire crust.

Insert slicing disk. Place tomato halves in feed tube vertically and slice. Arrange around edge of tuna. Bake 10-12 minutes or until heated through. Slice with sharp knife or pizza cutter.

Serves 4 as a main dish.

Potatoes,
Rice
and
Pasta

Curried Rice Salad

2 tomatoes, peeled, seeded, quartered
1 green pepper, halved with flat bottom
1 rib celery, cut into 1/2" lengths
1/4 cup parsley leaves
2 tbs. oil
1 tsp. curry powder
2 tsp. wine vinegar
1 tsp. chutney
2 tbs. raisins
2 cups cold cooked rice
salt and pepper
lettuce

Insert steel blade. Mince parsley. Set aside. Chop tomatoes with 2-3 quick on/off turns. Set aside. Chop celery with 3-4 on/off turns. Set aside. **Insert slicing disk.** Stand pepper halves in feed tube and slice using firm pressure.

Combine oil, vinegar, curry powder and chutney. Toss tomatoes, raisins, pepper, celery and parsley with the rice. Combine with oil and vinegar mixture. Season to taste with salt and pepper.

Serve in lettuce lined bowl or from individual molds.

Serves 4.

Spiced Turkish Rice

1/4 cup butter or margarine
3 medium onions, quartered
1/4 cup walnuts
2 cups uncooked long grain rice (not instant)
1 large fresh tomato, peeled and seeded,
    or 1 large canned tomato
1/4 cup raisins
2 tbs. salt
1/2 tsp. pepper (or more to taste)
1/2 tsp. ground sage
1/4 tsp. ground allspice
4 cups boiling beef boullion (from cubes or granules)

Insert steel blade. Chop raisins. Set aside. Chop nuts. Set aside. Chop onions coarsely using 2-3 on/off turns. Chop tomato using 2 on/off turns.

Melt butter and cook onion until soft but not brown. Add nuts and rice and cook over medium heat 5 minutes, stirring constantly. Add tomato, raisins, spices and boullion. Dish will sizzle. Stir thoroughly and cover tightly. Cook over low heat until rice is tender and liquid is absorbed, 20-30 minutes. Let stand covered 10 minutes before serving.

Garnish with chopped parsley or mint if desired.

Serves 6-8.

Rice and Pecan Loaf

1 cup pecans   Serves 6.
1 rib celery
1 medium onion
1 small carrot, cut in 3 pieces
1 cup cooked rice
1 cup dry herb stuffing mix
2 eggs
1/3 cup soft butter
1 cup tomato juice
1 cup water
1/2 tsp. caraway seed

Insert steel blade. Chop pecans with 4 on/off turns. Place in bowl. Chop celery using 3-4 on/off turns. **Insert shredding disk.** Grate onions and carrot into workbowl. Add vegetables to mixing bowl.

Combine with remaining ingredients. Let stand 2 hours, stirring several times. Pack into a greased 9" x 5" x 3" loaf pan. Bake at 300° for 1 hour or until firm. Unmold and serve.

Confetti Rice Salad

2 cups cooked rice
1 - 10 oz. package frozen peas, cooked and drained
1 medium zucchini, cut in half
2 roasted peppers or pimentoes
2/3 cup oil
3 tbs. cider vinegar
1/2 tsp. salt
1/4 tsp. sugar
1/4 tsp. basil

Combine rice and peas in mixing bowl.

Insert shredding disk and shred zucchini. Add to mixing bowl. Wipe bowl.

Insert steel blade and chop pimentoes. Add to bowl. Wipe bowl.

Insert plastic blade. Add remaining ingredients and mix. Toss with rice mixture.

Chill several hours. Serve on lettuce leaves or in tomato shells.

Layered Potato Bake

5 medium potatoes, peeled
1/4 tsp. salt
1/4 tsp. pepper
1 lb. mushrooms
1/4 lb. Jarlsberg or Gruyere cheese, cut into 1-1/2" cubes
1 small bunch parsley, stems removed
1 medium onion, quartered
2 cups heavy cream
1/2 cup butter

Preheat oven to 375°.

Insert steel blade. Place cheese in workbowl and process until finely grated. Set aside. Mince parsley, set aside.

Without cleaning bowl, add onion and chop, using 3 on/off turns. Set aside. Dry bowl. **Insert slicing disk** and pour cleaned mushrooms into the feed tube, one cup at a time, and slice using firm pressure. Set aside. Slice potatoes using medium pressure.

Rub a 2 qt. casserole with a cut clove of garlic and butter it well. Place a layer of potatoes on the dish, then a layer of mushrooms. Sprinkle with cheese, parsley, and onion, salt and pepper. Repeat layers until supply is used, ending with a layer of potatoes. Save 1/4 cup cheese. Cover the top layer with cream, then reserved cheese, and dot with butter. Bake 45 minutes or until potatoes are easily pierced.

6 - 8 servings.

Potato Kugel

4 medium potatoes, cubes
1 large onion, quartered
3 eggs
1-1/2 tsp. salt
1/4 tsp. pepper
1/4 cup chicken fat or butter
1/3 cup flour

Preheat oven to 350°.

Insert shredding disk. Pour potato cubes 1 cup at a time in the feed tube. Shred, using light pressure on the pusher. Grate onion. Place potato and onion in mixing bowl.

Insert plastic blade. Place eggs in workbowl, mix thoroughly. Add eggs and remaining ingredients to mixing bowl. Fold ingredients together. Pour into greased 8" square baking pan.

Bake for one hour.

Serves 6.

Old Fashioned Potato Pancakes

4 large potatoes, cut into 1-1/2" cubes
1 large onion, cut in 1/8's
1 egg
1/2 tsp. salt
dash pepper
1/3 cup matzoh meal or flour
salad oil

Insert steel blade. Chop potatoes, two at a time using on/off turns until they are very fine. Pour into mixing bowl. Add onions to the workbowl and chop, using about 5-6 on/off turns until pieces are very fine. Add to potatoes. Place egg in workbowl and turn on/off once. Add to potatoes. Add salt, pepper and enough matzoh meal or flour to bind the mixture (it should resemble cooked oatmeal).

Heat 1/8" - 1/4" of oil in a skillet or electric fry pan until very hot. Drop batter into oil with a large serving spoon. Fry until crisp and brown on one side, then turn over and cook on the second side. Drain on paper towels.

These pancakes can be reheated in a 425° oven. Place on a broiling pan so the excess oil is not absorbed.

The pancakes can be frozen after cooling. Reheat, frozen or defrosted in a 425° oven until oil bubbles.

Orange Baked Sweet Potatoes

3 lb. sweet potatoes, cooked and peeled
1 cup pecans
2 eggs
3/4 cup brown sugar
1/2 cup melted butter
1/2 tsp. cinnamon
1 tsp. salt
1 cup fresh orange juice
8 large orange shells
miniature marshmallows

Insert shredding disk. Grate pecans. Wedge pieces of potato in feed tube and grate. Pour nuts and potatoes into mixing bowl. Add butter, sugar, eggs, cinnamon and salt. Blend well. Add enough of 1 cup orange juice to moisten.

Slice tops off oranges, remove pulp. Fill shells with potato mixture and refrigerate until meal time. Bake at 375° for 20 minutes.

If desired, place marshmallows on top and place under broiler until browned. Watch carefully.

French Fries

5 large potatoes
oil for deep frying

Insert slicing disk. Slice potatoes and drop in cold water. Drain and dry off. Heat oil to boiling. Drop in slices, one at a time. Cook until light brown. Drain and salt to taste.

Noodle Souffle

8 oz. fine noodles, cooked and drained
8 oz. cream cheese, cut in 1 oz. pieces
4 tsp. butter
3 eggs, separated
1 pint sour cream
2 tbs. sugar
juice of one lemon
1 tsp. vanilla
1 - 8-3/4 oz. can drained, crushed pineapple
1/3 cup golden raisins

Insert steel blade. Beat egg whites until stiff peaks form. Place in large mixing bowl. **With steel blade in place,** cream butter and sugar. Add cream cheese, yolks, sour cream, lemon juice and vanilla, turning on/off just until combined. Fold into egg whites. Add noodles, raisins and pineapple and fold in gently. Pour in greased 2-1/2 quart oblong casserole and bake at 300° for 75 minutes.

Millie's Amazing Noodle Pudding

1 lb. wide noodles, parboiled and drained
2 tart apples, halved
8 eggs
3 cups orange juice
1 cup sugar
1 tsp. salt
2 tsp. lemon juice
juice and pulp of one orange
1/4 lb. butter
1/4 cup slivered almonds
cinnamon and sugar

Preheat oven to 350°.

Melt butter in 11" x 17" roasting pan. Pour cooked noodles in pan and toss with butter.

Insert grating disk. Using firm pressure, grate apple. Sprinkle lemon juice over apple. Set aside. **Insert plastic blade.** Place eggs in workbowl and beat until frothy. With machine still running, add sugar, salt, then orange juice. Pour mixture over noodles. Add apple and toss so that apple is incorporated. Sprinkle with cinnamon and sugar and slivered almonds. Bake 1 hour.

Spaghetti with Parsley — Walnut Sauce

3 cups parsley sprigs
1 cup walnuts
3 cloves garlic
2 oz. Parmesan cheese, cut in small cubes
1 tsp. salt
1 tsp. basil
1 cup olive oil
1 lb. spaghetti, cooked and drained
additional walnuts for garnish

Insert steel blade. Process cheese until powdery. Set aside. Place 2 tbs. cheese and all but last 2 ingredients in workbowl and process until smooth. Pour over hot spaghetti and toss. Garnish with additional nuts and remaining parmesan.

Serves 6.

Vegetables

Stuffed Mushrooms

12 large mushroom caps, reserve stems
1 tbs. olive oil
1 small onion, halved
1 small clove garlic
1/4 cup parsley leaves
1 slice white bread
1 egg
1/4 tsp. salt
dash pepper
2 tbs. bread crumbs

Preheat oven to 400°.

Insert steel blade. Process bread until large crumbs form. Place in bowl. Toss with 2 tbs. cold water and squeeze out excess liquid.

Reinsert steel blade. Place onion and garlic in workbowl and chop, turning on/off 3 times. Heat oil in skillet and add onion and garlic. Chop stems, turning on/off 2-3 times. Add to skillet and saute with onions and garlic. Wipe bowl.

Reinsert steel blade. Process parsley until minced. Add parsley, salt and pepper to skillet and saute several minutes more. Add mixture to bread crumbs.

Insert plastic blade. Mix egg. Add to other ingredients and toss lightly. Stuff mushrooms and sprinkle with additional bread crumbs. Drizzle with oil and bake in greased pan for 20 minutes.

Mushrooms A La Russe

1-1/2 lb. mushrooms, cleaned and trimmed
1 small onion
3 tbs. butter
3/4 cup water
2 tbs. flour
1 tsp. paprika
2/3 cup sour cream
3/4 cup light cream

Insert slicing disk. Pile mushrooms in feed tube and slice. **Insert shredding disk.** Grate onion. Saute onion and mushrooms in butter for 3 minutes. Add water and simmer, uncovered, until tender. Blend flour and paprika with sour cream and light cream. Cook stirring, until thick. Add mushrooms and liquid. Add salt and pepper to taste and simmer 5 minutes more.

Serves 8.

Chilled Filled Artichokes

6 large artichokes
fresh lemon juice
1 cup garlic mayonnaise

Wash, drain and trim tops and bottoms of artichokes. Remove small leaves from base and thorny tips from outer leaves. Rub cut edges with lemon juice. Press cut end firmly to separate leaves. Using a melon baller, scoop out center leaves and fuzzy core. Cover and simmer for 40 minutes. Drain, cover with plastic wrap and chill for 1 hour or more. Fill with Garlic Mayonnaise. Sprinkle with paprika.

GARLIC MAYONNAISE

1 egg
1/2 tsp. salt
1 tbs. vinegar
1/2 tsp. dry mustard
1/8 tsp. black pepper
1 cup oil
1 scallion top
1 clove garlic
few sprigs parsley

Insert steel blade. Add egg, salt, mustard and pepper. Process 10 seconds. With machine running, add vinegar. Pour oil in slowly as mixture thickens, drop in garlic, parsley and scallion top. Process until blended. Fill centers of chilled artichokes with mayonnaise.

Celery Souffle Ring

3 large ribs of celery, cut in 1-1/2" pieces (1-1/2 cup chopped)
1/2 large green pepper, cut in 1-1/2" pieces
1 small bunch parsley, stems removed
1 medium onion, quartered
2 pieces toasted bread, broken
3/4 cup pecans
1 cup milk
4 eggs
salt and pepper

Preheat oven to 350°.

Insert steel blade. Chop nuts using 3-4 on/off turns. Place in mixing bowl. Process bread crumbs until fine. Measure 1 cup and add to bowl. Mince parsley; add to bowl. Chop onion and celery pieces until very fine, about 4-5 on/off turns. Add to bowl. Chop pepper using 2-3 on/off turns or until finely minced. Add to bowl.

Separate eggs. **Insert plastic blade.** Add yolks and milk. Process until combined. Add to vegetables in the bowl. Mix all the ingredients well. Add salt and pepper to taste. Wash and dry bowl and blade thoroughly.

Reinsert steel blade. Beat egg whites until stiff peaks form. Fold whites into vegetables very gently.

Pour into a well greased 6 cup ring mold. Place mold in a pan of water. Bake for 1-1/2 hours. Unmold and fill with carrots or another contrasting food.

Serves 8.

*You may want to use an electric mixer to get greater volume with your egg whites.

Zucchini Pancakes

3 small zucchini, peeled, cut in 2" lengths
2 eggs
2 scallions or 1/2 large onion
1/2 cup mint leaves
1/2 cup parsley
2 oz. gruyere cheese
1/2 cup flour
salt and pepper
1 - 1-1/2 cup oil

Insert shredding disk. Using light pressure grate zucchini. Drain, salt and squeeze out liquid. Place in mixing bowl.

Insert steel blade. Mince mint leaves and parsley. Place in mixing bowl. Add cheese to bowl and process until finely grated. Add to mixing bowl. Add scallions or onions to workbowl and chop using on/off turns. Add to mixing bowl. Mix egg in workbowl; add to mixing bowl. Add flour gradually. Season to taste. Heat oil in large skillet. Drop by tablespoons. Fry on both sides. Drain.

Zucchini Rice Casserole

3 oz. parmesan cheese, cut in 1/2" pieces
2-1/2 lb. zucchini, cut into 3" lengths
2 medium onions
2 lb. fresh spinach or 2 - 10 oz. packages frozen spinach
2 cloves garlic
1/2 cup raw rice
4 tbs. oil
1 tbs. butter
2 tbs. flour
milk
salt and pepper

Insert shredding disk. Stand zucchini in feed tube and shred, using light pressure. Salt zucchini and drain over bowl. Dry workbowl.

Insert steel blade. Process cheese until powdery. Set aside. **Reinsert steel blade,** add onions and garlic and chop using 3 on/off turns.

Cook rice according to package directions. Saute onions in oil and butter until almost tender. Add spinach, cook until wilted. Stir in flour. Add enough milk to zucchini juices to measure 1-1/2 cups liquid. Cook and stir until thickened. Add cooked rice and zucchini and all but 3 tbs. cheese, salt and pepper to taste. Pour into greased baking dish and sprinkle with remaining cheese. Bake at 425° for 25-30 minutes or until bubbly and light brown.

Ratatouille

1/4 cup olive oil
1 medium unpeeled eggplant, quartered lengthwise
1 medium zucchini, cut in half
1 large green pepper, quartered lengthwise
1 large onion, quartered
1 - 1 lb. can tomatoes or 3 peeled fresh tomatoes
2 large cloves garlic
1/4 tsp. basil
1/2 tsp. oregano
1 tbs. vinegar
1 tbs. sugar
1/2 tbs. salt
1/8 tsp. pepper

Insert steel blade and with machine running drop garlic through feed tube and mince. Place onion in workbowl and chop coarsely using 2-3 on/off turns. Remove onion and garlic and place in large skillet with heated olive oil. Saute slowly while slicing remaining vegetables.

Insert slicing disk.* Stand vegetable pieces up vertically in feed tube and slicing using firm pressure for all of them. Add to skillet and toss. Add tomatoes and liquid, then seasonings. Cover pan and cook 20-25 minutes, remove cover and cook 10 minutes or until vegetables are tender and excess liquid is reduced. Serve warm or cold.

If you serve this as an appetizer, chop the vegetables coarsely instead of slicing them. Serve cold with crackers.

*Try using the American Electric wide slicing disk.

Baked Carrot Ring

1 lb. carrots, cut in 1-1/2" pieces
1 cup shortening
1/2 cup light brown sugar, firmly packed
1 large egg
1-1/4 cup sifted flour
1 tsp. cinnamon
1 tsp. baking powder
1-1/2 tsp. baking soda
1/2 tsp. salt

Preheat oven to 350°.

Insert steel blade. Chop carrots finely. Set aside. Place shortening and brown sugar in workbowl and process until creamed. Add egg and carrots and turn on/off until combined. Resift flour with other dry ingredients and put in workbowl. Turn on/off 3-4 times or just until combined. Spoon mixture into greased 5-1/2-6 cup ring mold and bake 30 minutes. Unmold and fill center with cooked peas.

String Bean Souffle

1 oz. parmesan cheese, cut into bits
1/2 lb. string beans, cut in half
1 medium onion
salt and pepper
1/8 tsp. mace
5 tbs. butter
1 tbs. flour
1 - 2/3 cup milk
4 eggs, separated

Insert steel blade. Process cheese until finely grated. Reserve 1/2 of cheese for a later time.

Chop onion with 3 on/off turns. Set aside. **Insert slicing disk.** Wedge beans in feed tube and slice. Heat 3 tbs. butter in saucepan and saute beans, onion, salt and pepper until onions are golden.

In another saucepan make a roux with 2 tbs. butter and 1 tbs. flour; add milk and mace gradually. Add bean mixture, cheese and egg yolks. **Insert steel blade** and puree mixture. Cool slightly.

Clean steel blade and bowl thoroughly. Beat egg whites until stiff. Fold whites into cooled bean mixture.

Heavily butter a 5 cup ring mold and place a piece of buttered waxed paper on the bottom. Place the mixture in the mold and set it in a pan of simmering water. Bake at 350° for 35-40 minutes or until top is firm. Serve with tomato or bechamel sauce.

Stuffed Tomatoes

4 ripe tomatoes
salt and pepper
1/2 slice stale bread
1 clove garlic
1/2 cup parsley leaves
2 scallions, cut to 6" lengths
1/8 tsp. thyme
3 tbs. olive oil
2 tbs. butter

Cut tomatoes in half, cut out pulp, sprinkle with salt and pepper, and turn over to drain.

Insert steel blade. Process bread until fine crumbs form. Pour into small bowl. **Replace blade.** Turn machine on, drop in garlic then scallions and parsley leaves. Process turning on/off until vegetables are minced. Add to bread crumbs. Sprinkle olive oil over and toss. Fill tomatoes and dot with small pieces of butter. Bake on oiled pan 15 minutes.

Serves 4.

Salads
and
Dressings

Chunky Tomato Salad

2 large ripe tomatoes, cut in chunks
1/2 Bermuda onion cut up
1 cucumber peeled and seeded, cut into 1-1/2" chunks
2 ribs celery, cut into 1-1/2" chunks
1/4 cup parsley leaves
12 pitted black olives
1/2 cup olive oil
1/4 cup wine vinegar
1 tsp. salt
1/8 tsp. pepper
1/8 tsp. garlic powder
1/4 tsp. oregano

Cut tomatoes by hand and place in mixing bowl. **Insert steel blade** and chop cucumber with very fast on/off turns. Leave the pieces quite chunky. Add to mixing bowl. Chop onion and celery together using 3 on/off turns. Add to bowl. Dry bowl and blade.

Insert steel blade. Mince parsley and add to bowl. Add olives to bowl.

Insert plastic blade. Add remaining ingredients and mix. Pour over vegetables and toss until coated. Chill before serving.

Serves 4-6.

Claremont Salad

1 whole cabbage cut into wedges
2 green peppers quartered
2 cucumbers, halved
2 carrots, cut in thirds
1 medium onion halved
3/4 cup sugar
1 cup white vinegar
1/3 cup water
1/2 cup oil
1 tbs. salt
2 cloves garlic

Insert slicing disk and slice cabbage with firm pressure, emptying bowl when necessary. Slice peppers with firm pressure. Add to cabbage. Slice cucumber using light pressure and add to vegetables. Wedge carrots in feed tube and slice using firm pressure.

Insert shredding disk and grate onion. Add to vegetables.

Insert steel blade. Turn machine on, drop garlic cloves through feed tube and mince. Add sugar, vinegar, water and salt and whirl. Place vegetables in large leakproof container. Pour liquid over and toss. Marinate overnight, turning bowl and vegetables several times.

Serves a crowd.

Easy Relish

1/3 of a small head of cabbage
2 green tomatoes, cut in quarters
2 large onions, cut in half
1 cucumber, cut to fit feed tube
1 medium red or green pepper, seeded and quartered

Insert slicing disk. Cut cabbage into wedges that will fit feed tube. Use light pressure when slicing. Wedge onions in feed tube and slice. Repeat with cucumber. Place sliced vegetables in saucepan.

Insert steel blade. Chop tomatoes coarsely. Add to saucepan. Wipe bowl. Repeat with green pepper. Add to saucepan.

Bring contents to a boil, reduce heat and simmer 30 minutes. Pour into hot sterilized jar. Seal and cool. Store in refrigerator.

Makes 2 pints.

Minted Fruit Coleslaw

1 large head cabbage
2 medium apples, peeled and cut into 1-1/2" pieces
1 - 13-1/4 oz. can undrained pineapple tidbits
green food coloring
4 drops mint flavoring
1/4 cup sugar
1 tsp. salt
1 cup sour cream
2 tsp. lemon juice

Add green food coloring and mint flavoring to undrained pineapple tidbits. Refrigerate several hours or overnight.

Insert slicing blade. Wedge pieces of cabbage into the feed tube. Slice, using light pressure. Place in large serving bowl.

Insert steel blade. Chop apples using 3 on/off turns. Add to serving bowl.

Drain pineapple tidbits. Add pineapple, sour cream, sugar and lemon juice to serving bowl. Toss to combine. Serve immediately.

Mayonnaise

1 large egg
1/2 tsp. salt
1/2 tsp. dry mustard
1 tbs. vinegar
1 cup vegetable or blended oil

Insert steel or plastic blade. Place egg, salt and mustard in workbowl. Process 10 seconds. With machine running, add vinegar. Then pour oil in through the feed tube in a steady stream. The mayonnaise will start to form almost immediately. The longer the machine runs the thicker the mayonnaise will become.

After the mayonnaise has thickened you may add other ingredients such as garlic, dill, parsley or chives.

Honey Dressing

1/2 cup vinegar
1/4 cup sugar
1/4 cup honey
1 tsp. dry mustard
1 tsp. paprika
1 tsp. celery seeds
1/4 tsp. salt
1 tsp. onion juice
1 cup salad oil

Mix vinegar, sugar, honey, mustard and paprika in a small saucepan and boil 3 minutes. Cool. **Insert plastic blade.** Add boiled mixture and remaining ingredients to workbowl. Whirl until combined. Serve with fruit salads or with greens.

Russian Dressing

1 small onion, halved
1/4 of a green pepper, cut in pieces
5 pimento stuffed olives
1/2 cup mayonnaise
1 tbs. chili sauce
2 tbs. milk
2 tbs. lemon juice
1/4 tsp. salt
1 tbs. prepared horseradish

Insert steel blade. Add onion, pepper and olives. Mince, using 3-4 on/off turns. **Remove steel blade. Insert plastic blade.** Add remaining ingredients and whirl until combined. Do not remove cover until liquid has dripped back into bowl. Pour into serving dish and chill, covered.

Tabbouleh

1 cup bulgur (cracked wheat)
3 medium tomatoes, peeled and quartered
1 bunch scallions
1 cup parsley leaves
1/2 cup fresh mint leaves
1/4 cup olive oil
1/4 cup fresh lemon juice
1/2 tsp. salt
1/4 tsp. freshly ground black pepper
Romaine or leaf lettuce

Wash bulgur; place in large bowl and cover with boiling water and let stand 30 minutes.

Insert steel blade. Chop parsley and mint. Set aside. Chop tomatoes, using 2-3 on/off turns.

Insert slicing disk. Cut scallions into thirds and wedge into feed tube. Slice.

Drain bulgur thoroughly and squeeze dry with hands. Combine with chopped vegetables in a large bowl. **Insert plastic blade.** Beat oil, lemon juice and salt and pepper together. Pour over bulgur and stir until well blended.

Serve in lettuce lined salad bowl or with chunks of pita bread.

Cookies, Cakes and Desserts

Marmalade Bars

1 cup walnuts
1/2 cup pitted whole dates, chilled
3/4 cup orange marmalade
1 cup brown sugar, firmly packed
1/2 cup butter or margarine, cut into 4 pieces
2 eggs
1-3/4 cup flour
1 tsp. baking soda
1/2 tsp. salt
1 tsp. vanilla

Preheat oven to 350°.

Insert steel blade. Chop nuts with 3-4 on/off turns. Set aside. Dredge dates with flour. Place in workbowl and process, turning on/off until chopped. Combine with marmalade in a small bowl.

Reinsert steel blade. Place butter in workbowl with sugar and vanilla. Process until creamed. With machine operating, drop eggs through feed tube, one at a time.

Sift dry ingredients together. Add to workbowl and turn on/off only until combined. Add nuts and process until they are mixed.

Spread 2/3 of the mixture in an ungreased 13" x 9" x 2" pan. Top with date mixture. Drop remaining dough by spoonfuls evenly over date layer. Bake for 20-25 minutes. Cool in pan. Cut in bars.

Makes 24 large bars.

Oatmeal Squares

3/4 cup walnuts
1/4 lb. margarine, cut in 4 pieces
1/3 cup white sugar
1/3 cup brown sugar
1/2 tsp. vanilla
1 large egg
1-1/4 cup flour
1 tsp. baking soda
1/4 tsp. salt
3/4 cup quick cooking oatmeal
1/3 cup chocolate chips

Preheat oven to 375°.

Insert steel blade. Add nuts to bowl and chop coarsely, using 2 on/off turns. Set aside.

Replace blade. Add margarine to bowl. Pour sugars, eggs and vanilla over and cream until smooth. Add dry ingredients and combine with several on/off turns. Sprinkle nuts and chips over dough and turn on/off until combined. Pour into a greased 9" x 13" x 2" pan, and spread evenly. Bake 15 minutes. Cool and cut into squares.

Maple Nut Bars

BOTTOM LAYER

1/2 cup butter
1/2 cup light brown sugar, packed
1 cup flour

TOPPING

2 cups walnuts, halved
1 cup sugar
1/2 tsp. maple flavoring
4 unbeaten egg whites

Preheat oven to 300°.

Insert steel blade. Cut butter into 4 pieces and place on blade. Pour sugar over. Process until creamed, scraping down sides. Add flour and turn on/off until combined. Scrape down flour from the sides. Press into greased 9″ square pan. Bake 20 minutes. Remove and let dough set 2-3 minutes. Set oven to 350°.

Clean bowl and steel blade. **Replace steel blade.** Pour nuts into workbowl and turn on/off 2-3 times, leaving nuts coarsely chopped. Place nuts and remaining ingredients in heavy saucepan and cook over low heat until mixture starts to thicken — about 5 minutes. Spread over bottom layer and return to oven and bake 20 minutes more. Cool and cut into squares.

Glazed Almond Cookies

3/4 cup blanched almonds
1/2 lb. butter, cut in 8 pieces
1 cup sugar
2 eggs, separated
2-2/3 cups sifted cake flour
1/2 tsp. salt
1/2 tsp. vanilla
1/2 tsp. almond extract
48 whole blanched almonds

Preheat oven to 350°.

Insert steel blade. Chop nuts, using on/off turns until pieces are fine. Set aside.

With steel blade in place, cream butter and sugar until light. With machine running add egg yolks and extracts. Add flour and nuts, blend just until combined.

Roll into 1″ balls, dip into unbeaten egg whites and place 2″ apart on greased cookie sheets. Push a whole almond in the center of each cookie and press down to flatten. Bake for 10 minutes.

Makes 4 dozen.

The Ultimate Chocolate Mousse

1-1/2 cups heavy cream, chilled
6 oz. semi-sweet chocolate chips
1/3 cup sugar
1/4 cup water
3 egg yolks
2 tbs. rum or orange liqueur
1/4 cup toasted slivered almonds

In small saucepan combine sugar and water and boil several minutes until a syrup appears. Keep hot.

Chill workbowl and steel blade for 10 minutes. Add chilled cream to bowl and process until thick, about 1-2 minutes. After cream thickens remove pusher to allow air to enter the workbowl. (Cream is whipped when no liquid falls back toward the blade when the motor is turned off). Scrape cream into mixing bowl. It is not necessary to wash workbowl.

Replace steel blade. Place chocolate chips in bowl. Turn machine on and process for about 10 seconds, then add hot sugar syrup and process until mixture becomes smooth.

Scrape down sides of bowl and continue to process. With machine running add egg yolks and rum or liqueur. Add nuts, and turn on/off about 5-6 times to chop. Pour chocolate mixture over whipped cream and fold together until white patches are gone.

Chill several hours.

Serves 4.

Cinnamon Ripple Brownies

1 cup nuts
1/2 lb. butter
2 squares unsweetened chocolate
2 cups sugar
4 eggs
2 tsp. vanilla
1-1/2 cups flour
1/2 tsp. salt
3/4 tsp. baking powder

RIPPLE FILLING
1-8 oz. package cream cheese, cut in cubes
1/4 cup sugar
3/4 tsp. cinnamon
1 egg
1-1/2 tsp. vanilla

Preheat oven to 350°.

Insert steel blade. Chop nuts coarsely, using 2-3 on/off turns. Set aside. Add filling ingredients to workbowl and whirl until smooth. Set aside. Wash and dry bowl.

Heat butter and chocolate over low heat until melted. Cool.

Insert steel blade. Place eggs in workbowl and beat. Add sugar through feed tube and beat until color changes. Add chocolate and process. Add dry ingredients and process until combined, turning on/off to combine flour. Add nuts and vanilla. Process until mixed.

Grease a 9" x 13" x 2" pan. Pour half the batter in the pan. Spread filling over batter. Spread remaining batter over filling. Swirl batter if desired. Bake 40-45 minutes, or until a tester comes out clean. Cool and cut into 1-1/2" squares.

Makes 64.

7-4-91
Apple Nut Crumb Pie

5 to 7 tart apples, peeled, cored and halved
1 - 9" unbaked pie shell
1/2 cup sugar
1 tsp. cinnamon
1/2 cup sugar
3/4 cup flour
1/3 cup butter or margarine, cut into 3 pieces
1/2 cup chopped walnuts or pecans

Insert shredding disk. Grate nuts using very firm pressure. Remove nuts and set aside 1/4 cup. Sprinkle remaining 1/4 cup nuts over the bottom of the pie shell.

Insert slicing disk and wedge apples in feed tube vertically. Slice with firm pressure. Place in large bowl. Combine cinnamon and sugar and toss with apples. Mound in pie shell.

Insert steel blade. Place butter on blades. Sprinkle flour and sugar over butter and turn on/off several times until crumbly. Sprinkle nuts over mixture and whirl until combined. Sprinkle topping over apples. Bake at 400° for 40-45 minutes.

Cool on a rack.

Porcupine Date Cookies

3/4 cup pitted dates, refrigerated
2 cups walnuts
1/2 cup sweet butter, cut into 4 pieces
3/4 cup sugar
1 egg
1/2 tsp. vanilla
1-1/4 cup flour
1/2 tsp. baking soda
1/2 tsp. salt

Preheat oven to 350°.

Insert steel blade. Place 1 cup nuts in workbowl and chop, using 3-4 on/off turns. Set aside. Add remaining 1 cup nuts, turn on/off several times, then let machine run until nuts are finely chopped, but not ground. Set aside.

Dredge dates with flour, place in workbowl **with steel blade.** Chop the dates using about 5 on/off turns. Set aside.

Reinsert steel blade. Place butter on blade. Pour sugar over and process until creamed. With the machine running add the egg and the vanilla through the feed tube. Combine dry ingredients and add to workbowl. Process, turning on/off several times just until flour is combined. Add dates and coarsely chopped nuts; turn on/off several times until combined. **Remove blade from bowl.** Pour remaining nuts into a shallow dish. Form dough into 1" balls, then roll in finely chopped nuts until completely covered. Place 2" apart on ungreased cookie sheets. Bake 13-15 minutes or until lightly browned. Cool slightly and remove from sheets.

Makes 36.

Ruggelach

DOUGH

8 oz. *lightly salted butter, cut in 8 pieces*
8 oz. *cream cheese, cut in cubes*
2 cups sifted flour

FILLING

4 egg whites, at room temperature
2 cups walnuts
1/2 cup sugar
1 tsp. cinnamon
1/2 cup golden raisins

Insert steel blade. Place butter and cream cheese in workbowl and process until combined. Add flour and turn on/off until flour is incorporated. Some pieces may remain loose; just work them into the dough with your fingers. Roll dough into a large rectangle on a floured board. Fold in thirds, wrap in waxed paper and chill overnight.

Preheat oven to 375°.

Insert steel blade. Place egg whites in bowl and process until stiff, several minutes. Place in mixing bowl. Wash and dry workbowl.

Insert grating disk. With cover in place, pour 1 cup nuts into feed tube and grate, using firm pressure. Repeat, using remaining nuts. Add nuts to egg whites. Add cinnamon, sugar and raisins and fold ingredients together gently.

Break off a portion of the chilled dough, and roll it out to a circle on a floured board. Cut into pie wedges. Spread small amount of filling on wide end of each wedge, about 1" from the edge, fold over, tuck in sides and roll toward the point. Sprinkle a mixture of cinnamon and sugar over cookies and bake 20 minutes.

Sheila's Incredible Brownies

1/2 lb. sweet butter
4 oz. unsweetened chocolate
4 eggs
2-1/4 cups sugar
2 tsp. vanilla
1 cup sifted flour
1 - 12 oz. package semi-sweet chocolate chips

Preheat oven to 350°.

Melt chocolate and butter over low heat or in the top part of a double boiler. Cool.

Insert steel blade. Place eggs in workbowl and process until frothy. With the machine running, slowly add sugar through the feed tube. Let the machine run several minutes or until the mixture is thick and lighter in color. Add vanilla, flour and turn on/off just until combined. Add chocolate mixture and process until combined. Add chocolate chips and turn on/off several times until mixed.

Pour into greased 9" x 13" x 2" pyrex pan and bake 25-30 minutes. Cool before cutting.

Betty Browns

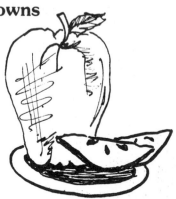

4 small Macintosh apples
  (2 cups sliced)
1/2 cup nuts
1/2 cup margarine, cut in 4 pieces
1 cup sugar
1 egg
1 cup flour
1/2 tsp. baking powder
1/2 tsp. baking soda
1/4 tsp. salt
1 tsp. cinnamon

Preheat oven to 350°.

Insert steel blade. Place nuts in workbowl and chop coarsely using 3 on/off turns.

Peel, core and quarter apples lengthwise. **Insert slicing disk.** Wedge apple pieces in feed tube and slice, using medium pressure. Set aside.

Reinsert steel blade. Place butter in workbowl. Pour sugar over and cream. Add egg and whirl until combined. Add dry ingredients and turn on/off only until combined. Add apples and nuts and turn on/off only until incorporated. Spread batter in greased 9" square pan. Bake 35-40 minutes or until tester comes out clean. Cool and sprinkle with confectioners sugar.

Basic 9" One Shell Pie Crust

1/4 lb. frozen butter, cut into 5 or 6 pieces
1-1/2 cup flour
1/2 tsp. salt
4 tbs. ice water

Insert steel blade. Place butter on blade. Pour flour and salt over. Turn on/off until fine crumbs form, about 7 or 8 turns. Turn machine on, remove pusher, and slowly add water to workbowl. As soon as a ball begins to form over the blade, about 15 seconds, turn the machine off. Gather up loose pieces of dough and press them into the ball. (Do not process until these small pieces are picked up or you will have a tough pastry).

This dough is ready to be rolled. If you are using it for a fruit pie it can be filled immediately. If you are going to prebake it, chill it for 1 hour to eliminate shrinking. Prick before prebaking.

Strawberry Bavarian

1 quart ripe strawberries, washed and hulled
2 envelopes unflavored gelatin
1/3 cup orange juice
3/4 cup sugar
2 cups heavy cream, chilled
1 package ladyfingers
whole berries for garnish
mint leaves

Place orange juice in a 1 cup measure. Sprinle gelatin over juice and allow to soften 5 minutes. Then place in pan of simmering water and stir until dissolved. Cool.

Insert steel blade. Place 1/2 of berries in workbowl and process until all lumps are gone. As large pieces disappear, add remaining berries through feed tube and continue processing until a thick puree appears. Add sugar and gelatin and whirl until combined. Pour into large bowl and chill until slightly thickened but not set, about 1/2 hour. Wash and dry bowl and blade and chill 10 minutes.

Insert steel blade. Pour cream into bowl and process until cream is completely whipped and no liquid remains on bottom of bowl. Scrape out and pour over partially set gelatin mixture. Fold two mixtures together gently until completely combined. Pour into an 8" spring form pan that has been lined with ladyfingers.

Garnish with whole berries and mint leaves and chill, several hours or overnight.

Serves 8-10.

All-In-One Filled Chocolate Roll

1 cup pecans
1/4 cup butter
1-1/3 cup flaked coconut
1 - 14 oz. can condensed milk
3 eggs
1 cup sugar
1/3 cup cocoa
2/3 cup flour
1/4 tsp. salt ⎬ *Sifted together*
1/4 tsp. baking soda
1/3 cup water
1 tsp. vanilla

Preheat oven to 375°. Line a 10" x 15" jelly-roll pan with foil. Melt the butter in the pan.

Insert steel blade. Chop nuts with 3-4 on/off turns. Sprinkle nuts over butter in pan. Sprinkle coconut over nuts. Drizzle with condensed milk.

Replace steel blade. Add eggs to workbowl and process for 15-20 seconds. Add sugar through feed tube and process until mixture changes color. With machine running, add water and vanilla. Process until blended. Remove cover. Sprinkle dry ingredients over egg mixture and process turning on/off until combined. Pour into prepared pan. Bake 20-25 minutes or until cake springs back when touched in the center.

Sprinkle cake with confectioner's sugar and cover with a lined dish towel. Place a second cookie sheet over the towel and invert. Remove pan and slowly peel off foil. Starting with the 10" side roll up, jelly roll fashion using the towel to help roll cake. Trim ends on the diagonal. Keep wrapped in towel until ready to serve. Sprinkle with additional confectioner's sugar.

*Most rolled cakes crack on the side. Don't be concerned about a crack. The sugar will camoflage it.

Sour Cream Coffee Cake

2 tsp. baking powder
1 tsp. baking soda
pinch of salt
1 tsp. vanilla
1 tsp. lemon juice
1/2 cup butter, cut in 4 pieces
1/2 cup margarine, cut in four pieces
1 cup sugar
3 eggs
1 cup sour cream
2-1/2 cups sifted flour

TOPPING

1/2 cup chopped nuts
1/2 cup chocolate chips
1/2 cup sugar
1 tsp. cinnamon

Preheat oven to 375°.

Insert steel blade. Chop nuts using 3-4 on/off turns. Add cinnamon and sugar and whirl until combined. Set aside. Wipe bowl.

Insert steel blade. Place butter and margarine in workbowl. Pour sugar over and process until mixture is creamed. Continue processing and add eggs, one at a time through the feed tube. Add vanilla, lemon juice.

Sift dry ingredients together. Add dry ingredients alternately with sour cream, whirling only until combined each time. DON'T OVERPROCESS.

Pour 1/2 of the batter into a greased 10" tube pan. Combine chocolate chips with nut mixture and sprinkle 1/2 of the topping over the batter. Pour in remaining batter, then remaining topping.

Bake at 350° for 35-45 minutes. Cool in pan.

Beignets Souffle

1 cup water
4 tbs. butter, cut in pieces
1/4 tsp. salt
1 cup flour
4 eggs

Heat oil to 375°.

Place butter, salt and water in saucepan. Bring to a boil. Remove from heat as soon as butter is melted. Add flour all at once and beat with a wooden spoon until mixture forms a ball and pulls away from the side of the pan. Return to a low heat and stir 20-30 seconds.

Insert steel blade. Place the mixture in the workbowl. Turn machine on. Add eggs one at a time through the feed tube and process until smooth.

Drop mounded tablespoons of dough into hot oil and fry 3-5 minutes or until brown and crisp. Turn if necessary. As these cook, they will expand continuously. (If they are undercooked, they will have a heavy center). Drain on paper towels. Serve filled with pastry cream, confectioner's sugar or warmed preserves.

Mocha Nut Butter Balls

2 cups pecans or walnuts
1 cup butter
1/2 cup sugar
2 tsp. vanilla
2 tsp. instant coffee powder (not freeze dried)
1/4 cup cocoa
1-3/4 cup sifted flour
1/2 tsp. salt
confectioners sugar

Preheat oven to 325°.

Insert steel blade. Place nuts in workbowl and process, using on/off turns until finely chopped. Set aside.

Reinsert steel blade. Cut each stick of butter into 4 pieces and place on blade. Pour sugar over butter and process until mixture is creamed. Add dry ingredients together and process only until combined. Pour in reserved nuts and combine, using on/off turns.

Shape into 1" balls and place on ungreased cookie sheets. Bake for 15 minutes. Cool completely and roll in confectioner's sugar.

Makes 4 dozen.

7-4-91 = good

Upside Down Cheesecake Pie

1 - 9" unbaked pie shell, see page 121
1 - 8 oz. package cream cheese, cut in cubes
1 egg
1/3 cup sugar
1/2 tsp. vanilla
1 cup pecan halves

2 eggs
1/4 cup sugar
2/3 cup dark corn syrup
1/2 tsp. maple flavoring
1/4 tsp. vanilla

Preheat oven to 375°.

Insert steel blade. Place cream cheese on blade. Pour 1 egg, 1/3 cup sugar, 1/2 tsp. vanilla on top. Turn machine on/off until mixture is combined, scraping down the sides if necessary. Then process until smooth and creamy. Pour into pie shell. Sprinkle nuts over cream cheese mixture.

Wash bowl. **Insert plastic blade.** Mix eggs, then add remaining ingredients and process only until combined. Pour over pecans. Bake 40-45 minutes or until set. Serve lukewarm or chilled.

Serves 6-8.

7-10-91 = good FAIR

Peanut Butter Cake

used small bundt pan NO

1/4 cup butter
1/4 cup peanut butter
1 cup sugar
2 eggs
1-1/2 cup flour
1 tsp. baking soda   } *Sifted 3 times*
1-1/4 tsp. baking powder
1 cup buttermilk
1/2 tsp. vanilla

Insert steel blade. Place butter, peanut butter and sugar in workbowl and cream until smooth. With machine running, add eggs, then buttermilk. Pour in dry ingredients and turn machine on and off just until combined. Add vanilla and turn on/off once to combine. Pour into greased and floured 9" x 13" x 2" pan. Bake 45 minutes at 350°.

FROSTING

halved Frosting recipe!

4 oz. butter
1/2 cup peanut butter
1/2 lb. confectioner's sugar
1-1/2 tsp. vanilla
pineapple juice

Insert steel blade. Cream butter and peanut butter. Add sugar and vanilla and process until blended. Add juice a little at a time until a spreading consistency is achieved.

Marbled Brownies

1 cup walnuts
1 cup butter, cut into 8 pieces
3/4 cup granulated sugar
3/4 cup brown sugar, firmly packed
2-1/2 cups flour
1 tsp. baking soda
1 tsp. salt
2 eggs
1 tsp. vanilla
1 tsp. water
1 - 12 oz. package semi-sweet chocolate chips

Preheat oven to 375°.

Insert steel blade. Chop nuts using 2-3 quick on/off turns. Set aside.

Reinsert steel blade. Place pieces of butter in workbowl. Cover with sugars. Process until creamed. With machine running, add eggs, water and vanilla. Mix dry ingredients together and add to workbowl. Combine, using on/off turns until flour disappears. Sprinkle nuts and 1 cup of the chips over the batter and turn the machine on to combine. Spread batter in a greased 10" x 15" jelly roll pan. Sprinkle remaining chocolate chips over the batter. Place pan in oven for 1 minute. Remove from oven. Run the tines of a fork over the surface of the batter, pulling the melted chocolate in straight lines in both directions. Return pan to oven, bake for 20 minutes.

Apple Strudel

3 apples, peeled, cored and cut into 1-1/2" pieces
1/4 cup walnuts
1 - 2" slice of pound cake or 5 graham crackers
1/4 cup golden raisins
1 tbs. lemon juice
1/2 cup sugar
1 tsp. cinnamon
3 sheets phyllo or strudel dough. (See instructions for
    working with dough on page 13.
1/2 cup melted butter

Insert steel blade. Place nuts in workbowl and chop finely using 5-6 on/off turns. Set aside. Place cake or crackers in workbowl and process until fine crumbs form. Set aside. Place apples in workbowl and chop using 2-3 on/off turns. (Do not overchop or you will have applesauce). Place apples in large bowl and toss with lemon juice.

Apple Strudel - cont.

Combine cinnamon, sugar, nuts raisins and 1/4 cup crumbs. Toss with apples.

Spread one sheet of dough on waxed paper, long side parallel with the counter. Brush with melted butter and part of remaining crumbs. Repeat layer again. After spreading the third sheet, spoon drained apple mixture into a strip several inches wide, across the length of dough, 3-4 inches from the edge. Roll the edge over the filling, using the paper as an aid. Tuck in the sides, and roll leaves to the end, continuing to use the paper. Brush with melted butter and slide onto a buttered cookie sheet with sides.

Bake 35 minutes at 350-400° or until golden brown. Cut and serve while still warm.

The dough will become soft when cooled and when reheated will become crisp again.

Linzer Torte

1/2 lb. blanched almonds
2 hardboiled egg yolks, chilled
1 cup sweet butter, cut in 8 pieces
1 cup sugar
2 raw egg yolks
juice of one lemon

1 tbs. brandy
1/2 tsp. cinnamon
2 cups flour
1 tsp. baking powder
1 cup rasberry jam
confectioner's sugar

Insert steel blade. Place almonds in workbowl and process, turning on/off several times until well chopped. Then leave machine running until nuts are pulverized. Remove and set aside.

Insert steel blade. Pulverize egg yolks. Set aside. **With steel blade in place,** press butter on blades. Pour sugar over butter and cream mixture. Process briefly. Add reserved cooked yolks, raw yolks, brandy and lemon juice. Add flour, cinnamon, baking powder and almonds and process until combined. **Remove blade.** Press 3/4 of the dough into a greased 9" spring form pan, pushing the dough up the sides to form a shallow rim. Spread with 3/4 cup jam. Flatten remaining dough into 1/2" thick rectangle and chill 1 hour or until firm. Cut strips of chilled dough and roll into 3/8" strips long enough to reach side of pan. (Use floured board if dough is too sticky). Arrange strips in a lattice pattern over jam covered dough. Seal edges. Bake in preheated 350°oven 45-50 minutes or until pale gold in color. Before serving, fill spaces between strips with remaining jam. Sprinkle with confectioner's sugar. Cut in narrow wedges.

This freezes well.

Serves 10-12.

Disappearing Fruit Cake

1 cup sugar
1/2 cup butter, cut in 4 pieces
1 cup flour
1 tsp. baking powder
2 eggs
1 tsp. vanilla
1/8 tsp. salt
fresh fruit (1 pint blueberries or 4 sliced apples* or
    5 sliced peaches* or a combination)
1/2 cup sugar
1/2 tsp. cinnamon
1 tbs. lemon juice

Preheat oven to 350°.

Insert steel blade. Place butter on blade, pour sugar over and cream. Add eggs and dry ingredients and vanilla and process until smooth and creamy. Do not overprocess.

Pour into greased 8" or 9" spring form pan. Cover top of batter with fruit. Sprinkle with lemon juice (and flour if juicy fruit is used) and cinnamon and sugar mixture. Bake 1 hour. Serve warm with ice cream.

*Halve peaches or apples. Pit or core fruit. Stand halves in feed tube vertically and slice, using firm pressure.

Coffee Can Pumpkin Bread

1 cup walnuts
1-1/2 cup sugar
1/2 cup oil
2 eggs
1 cup canned pumpkin pie filling
1-3/4 cup sifted flour
1 tsp. baking soda
1-1/2 tsp. nutmeg
1-1/2 tsp. pumpkin pie spice
1-1/2 tsp. cinnamon
1/3 cup water
1 tsp. salt

Note: If you use Comstock pie filling cut down by 1/2 tsp. on each of the 3 spices.

Preheat oven to 350°.

Insert steel blade. Chop nuts coarsely, using 1 or 2 on/off turns. Set aside. **Replace steel blade.** Add sugar, oil, eggs, water and pumpkin. Process until smooth. Sift dry ingredients together and add to workbowl. Process until combined. Add walnuts and combine, using on/off turn until nuts are mixed into batter.

Grease 2 - 1 lb. coffee cans and place a round of waxed or brown paper on the bottom. Fill cans half way with batter. Bake for 1 hour. Cool 10 minutes on racks; remove from cans. Continue cooling. Wrap in plastic or foil. You may also use one 9" x 5" x 3" loaf pan.

These freeze well.

Praline Cheesecake

CRUST
 17 single graham crackers (1 cup crumbs)
 3 tbs. melted butter
 3 tbs. sugar

CAKE
 3/4 cup pecans
 3 - 8 oz. packages cream cheese, cut into cubes
 1-1/4 cups dark brown sugar, firmly packed
 3 eggs
 2 tbs. flour
 1-1/2 tsp. vanilla

Preheat oven to 350°.

Insert steel blade. Break up crackers in workbowl and process until fine crumbs form. Add sugar and melted butter. Combine using on/off turns. Press into bottom of 8" spring form pan. Bake 10 minutes. Cool in pan. Wash and dry bowl. **Insert steel blade.** Place nuts in workbowl and chop with 2 on/off turns. Set aside.

Place cream cheese on blade and pour sugar over. Process until combined, and then with machine running, add eggs, one at a time, then vanilla and flour. Stop machine. Add nuts, turn on/off only until combined. Pour into pan. Bake 55 minutes or until set. Leave oven door open and allow cake to cool two hours. Remove and chill. Brush top with maple syrup and garnish with additional chopped pecans.

Watermelon Freeze

2-1/2 cups watermelon chunks, seeded
1 envelope unflavored gelatin
1 cup sugar
2 tsp. lemon juice
1 cup heavy cream, chilled

Insert steel blade. Add watermelon chunks to bowl and puree. Measure 2-1/4 cups puree. Soften gelatin in 1/4 cup of the puree. Heat the remaining puree in a saucepan until almost boiling. Add the softened gelatin and stir until dissolved. Remove from heat. Add sugar and lemon juice. Chill, stirring occasionally until mixture mounds when dropped from a spoon.

Chill bowl and blade for 10 minutes. Whip cream and fold into puree. Pour into a 4 cup mold. Freeze. Unmold and garnish with mint sprigs.

Serves 6.

Chocolate Surprise Cake

1 - 8 oz. package dates (cold) 1 cup sugar
1/2 cup walnuts 1-3/4 cup sifted flour
1 cup boiling water 1/2 tsp. salt
1 tsp. baking soda 3 tbs. cocoa
1/2 cup butter 1 tsp. vanilla
1/2 cup shortening 1 - 6 oz. package chocolate chips
2 eggs 2-3 tbs. granulated sugar

Preheat oven to 350°.

Insert steel blade. Chop nuts, using 2-3 on/off turns. Set aside. Dredge dates with flour. Chop, using on/off turns until coarse pieces form. Combine dates in a small bowl with water and baking soda. Cool 10 minutes.

Reinsert steel blade. Cream butter, shortening, sugar and eggs. Sift dry ingredients together. Add to creamed mixture alternately with date mixture, using on/off turns after each addition. Add 1/2 cup chocolate chips to batter, combine with on/off turns. Pour into greased 9" x 13" x 2" pan. Sprinkle nuts, remaining chocolate chips and 2-3 tbs. granulated sugar over the top. Bake 35-45 minutes. DO NOT OVERBAKE.

Peach Kuchen

8 firm, ripe peaches, halved and pitted
1-1/2 cup flour
1/2 tsp. salt
1/2 cup butter or margarine, cut into 4 pieces
1/3 cup sour cream
3 egg yolks
1 cup sugar

Preheat oven to 375°.

Insert slicing disk. Stand peach halves vertically and slice using firm pressure. Set aside. Wipe bowl.

Insert steel blade. Place butter on blade. Pour flour and salt and 2 tbs. sour cream over butter and combine using 3-4 on/off turns. Mixture should be crumbly. Press mixture into bottom on 9" square or 10" spring form pan. Bake 20 minutes. Spread peaches on baked crust.

Wipe bowl. **Insert plastic blade.** Combine remaining sour cream, sugar and egg yolks and process 5 seconds or until combined. Pour over peaches. Bake 35-40 minutes or until firm. Serve lukewarm or chilled with ice cream.

TIP — Spray bottom and sides of pan with a non-stick spray. This cake tends to be difficult to remove from the pan.

Strawberry Fluff Puffs

CREAM PUFF SHELLS

1/2 cup butter or margarine
1 cup water
1 cup flour
1/4 tsp. salt
4 large eggs

Place butter, salt and water in saucepan. Bring to a boil. Remove from the heat and beat in flour all at once until completely blended. Return the mixture to heat and beat with a wooden spoon until the ingredients are thoroughly blended and mixture pulls away from side of the pan. **Insert steel blade.** Scrape batter into workbowl. Turn machine on and add eggs one at a time through the feed tube. Be sure each egg is incorporated before adding the next one. Mixture should be smooth and shiny. Drop by heaping tablespoons 3″ apart onto greased cookie sheet. Bake at 450° for 15 minutes, then 325° for 25 minutes. Cool, split and remove webbing.

STRAWBERRY FLUFF FILLING

1 quart strawberries, washed and hulled
2 cups miniature marshmallows
1/4 cup sugar
1 cup sour cream

Insert plastic blade. Crush 1 pint of berries with several on/off turns. **Insert slicing disk,** slice remaining berries. Combine and chill.

In a large bowl combine sour cream, marshmallows and sugar. Chill several hours. Then fold in reserved berries. Spoon 1/4 cup mixture into each shell. Spoon 1 tbs. on top.

Makes 10 puffs.

Cherry Crepes Jubilee

Prepare 1 recipe crepes (see page 86)
add 1 tbs. sugar
1 tbs. orange liqueur or vanilla

ALMOND FILLING

1/2 cup toasted almonds
1 cup sugar
1/4 cup flour
1 cup milk, scalded
2 eggs
2 egg yolks
3 tbs. butter
2 tsp. vanilla
1/2 tsp. almond extract

Insert steel blade. Place almonds in workbowl and chop finely. Set aside.

Insert steel blade. Place eggs and yolks in workbowl. Process until color changes slightly, then add sugar and flour through feed tube. Process until pale and foamy, then add scalded milk in a thin stream while machine is running.

Pour into saucepan (use a Flame Tamer if you have one) and cook, stirring vigorously with a whisk until the mixture begins to bubble. Immediately, reduce the heat, and cook stirring constantly for 2 or 3 minutes until thick. Remove from heat. Stir in butter, vanilla and almond extract. Fold in almonds. Cool uncovered or with plastic wrap directly on the filling.

BRANDIED CHERRY SAUCE

1 - 21 oz. can cherry pie filling
3 tbs. brandy
2 tbs. butter
1 tbs. lemon juice

Heat all ingredients together in saucepan.

Spread 1/4 cup filling on uncooked side of crepe. Roll up and place in baking dish. Brush with melted butter if desired. Bake 20-25 minutes at 350° or until heated through.

To serve, spoon cherry sauce on top of crepes. Heat 3-4 tbs. brandy in a small pan, flame, and pour over cherries.

Makes 8 crepes.

INDEX

Main Dishes

Beef

Chicken

Lamb

Veal

Noodles and Pasta

Pies

Potatoes

NEED MORE BOOKS?
WANT ONE SENT AS A GIFT?

Yes! Please send me

_____copies of **"INSIDE THE FOOD PROCESSOR"** at $5.00 plus $.75 postage and handling.

_____copies of **"ORIENTAL EXPRESS"** at $5.00 plus $.75 postage and handling.

(N.J. residents add 5% sales tax.)

_____Total enclosed.

Mail to:
Name _____

Street_____Apt.# _____

City, State & Zip _____

☐ Check here if this is a gift. Card with sender's name will be enclosed.

Please send check or money order to:

GOOD FOOD BOOKS
17 Colonial Terrace
Maplewood, New Jersey 07040

NEED MORE BOOKS?
WANT ONE SENT AS A GIFT?

Yes! Please send me

_____copies of **"INSIDE THE FOOD PROCESSOR"** at $5.00 plus $.75 postage and handling.

_____copies of **"ORIENTAL EXPRESS"** at $5.00 plus $.75 postage and handling.

(N.J. residents add 5% sales tax.)

_____Total enclosed.

Mail to:
Name _____

Street_____Apt.# _____

City, State & Zip _____

☐ Check here if this is a gift. Card with sender's name will be enclosed.

Please send check or money order to:

GOOD FOOD BOOKS
17 Colonial Terrace
Maplewood, New Jersey 07040

NEED MORE BOOKS?
WANT ONE SENT AS A GIFT?

Yes! Please send me

_____copies of **"INSIDE THE FOOD PROCESSOR"** at $5.00 plus $.75 postage and handling.

_____copies of **"ORIENTAL EXPRESS"** at $5.00 plus $.75 postage and handling.

(N.J. residents add 5% sales tax.)

_____Total enclosed.

Mail to:
Name _____

Street_____Apt. # _____

City, State & Zip _____

☐ Check here if this is a gift. Card with sender's name will be enclosed.

Please send check or money order to:

**GOOD FOOD BOOKS
17 Colonial Terrace
Maplewood, New Jersey 07040**

NEED MORE BOOKS?
WANT ONE SENT AS A GIFT?

Yes! Please send me

_____copies of **"INSIDE THE FOOD PROCESSOR"** at $5.00 plus $.75 postage and handling.

_____copies of **"ORIENTAL EXPRESS"** at $5.00 plus $.75 postage and handling.

(N.J. residents add 5% sales tax.)

_____Total enclosed.

Mail to:
Name _____

Street_____Apt. # _____

City, State & Zip _____

☐ Check here if this is a gift. Card with sender's name will be enclosed.

Please send check or money order to:

**GOOD FOOD BOOKS
17 Colonial Terrace
Maplewood, New Jersey 07040**